THE
Lost Lady
OF THE
Amazon

THE
Lost Lady
OF THE
Amazon

The Story of Isabela Godin and her Epic Journey

Anthony Smith

CONSTABLE • LONDON

Constable & Robinson Ltd
3 The Lanchesters
162 Fulham Palace Road
London W6 9ER
www.constablerobinson.com

First published in the UK by Constable
an imprint of Constable & Robinson Ltd 2003

A copy of the British Library Cataloguing in
Publication Data is available from the British Library

ISBN 1-84119-519-7

Printed and bound in the EU

Dedicated to the good and
hospitable people of
St Amand Montrond

and to John and André who
made it all such fun

A Elouilly près Ham 20 Oct. 1773. *Lettre de Monsieur de*

Sur le sort des astronomes qui ont été tués ...

Vous vous êtes intéressé, Monsieur, aux travaux ...
êtes curieux de savoir le sort de tous ceux qui ont ...
depuis 1735. Je pourrais vous répondre par ce ...
cette vaste mer, échappés au naufrage, on voit quelque ...
de la Rochelle au mois de Mai 1735, munis des ...
pour aller mesurer les degrés voisins de l'équateur ...
étions trois Académiciens, M. Godin, M. Bougu...
Docteur régent de la faculté de Paris, frère des deu...
absence ; M. Séniergues Chirurgien : & pour nous ...
M. de Morainville dessinateur pour l'Histoire naturell...
Horloger, Ingénieur en instruments de mathématique ...
Lieutenans de vaisseaux Espagnols, nommés par la C...
L'année suivante M. de Maupertius, chargé d'alle...
s'embarqua à Rouen avec M. M. Clairaut, Cam...
M. Celsius, Astronome Suédois, & quelques autres a...
pour le Cap de Bonne Espérance où le moindre de ses ...
cinq voyageurs qui ont vu le cercle polaire il ne rest...
voyage du Cap. & dont la santé paraissait à toute é...
tionomique, en 1762 ; & un Académicien plus jeu...
même sort en Californie f. M. l'abbé Chappe d'Auter...
Parmi mes compagnons de voyage à l'équateur, ...
arrivé à Quito, fut emporté en trois jours par une f...
notre Chirurgien. M. Bouguer est mort d'un abcès au f...

Jean Godin sent lengthy letters from Cayenne to his former leader, ...
ultimately the astonishing journey of his wife.

Condamine à M ***.

...adémie des Sciences pour la mesure de la terre, & vous

...à cet ouvrage dans des voyages au delà des mers,

...irgile : Apparent rari nantes in gurgite vasto. Dans

...ches se sauver à la nage. ... Nous partîmes

...ports de Sa majesté Catholique le Roi Philippe V,

...ses Etats de l'Amérique méridionale. Nous

...noi. Nous avions pour adjoints M. Joseph de Jussieu

...demiciens & qui fut reçu à l'Académie pendant son

...dans nos opérations, M. Verguin, Ingénieur de la Marine,

...: Couplet, neveu de l'Académicien et le sieur Hugo

...nous joignîmes, à Carthagène d'Amérique, à deux

...Madrid, pour assister à nos observations.

...urer les degrés du méridien sous le cercle polaire arctique

...le Monnier le cadet, académiciens, M. l'abbé Outhier

...x. En 1751, M. l'Abbé Caille académicien partit

...ux fut la mesure de deux degrés du méridien ... Des

...M. Le Monnier. L'Abbé de la Caille qui fit seul le

...e, de retour à Paris, a été la victime de son zèle as-

...e lui, qui l'avait pris pour modèle, a eu depuis le

...t en Californie après son observation du passage de Vénus sur le Soleil 1769.

...uplet, le plus robuste & l'un des plus jeunes, à peine

...maligne. J'ai rendu compte ailleurs de la fin tragique de

...1758; M. Godin qui avait passé au service de l'Espagne

xplaining first his own voyage, then his predicament, and

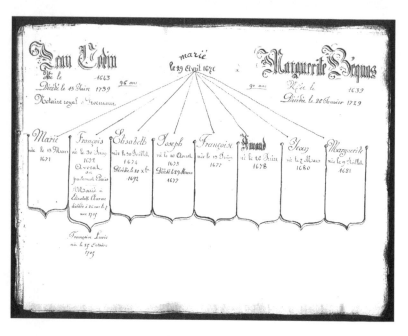

Godin Family Trees

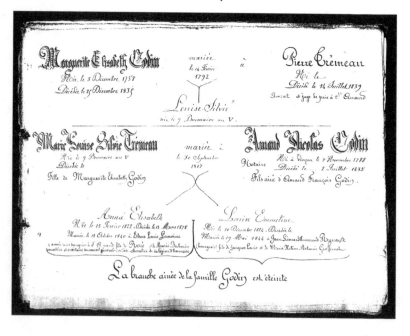

Contents

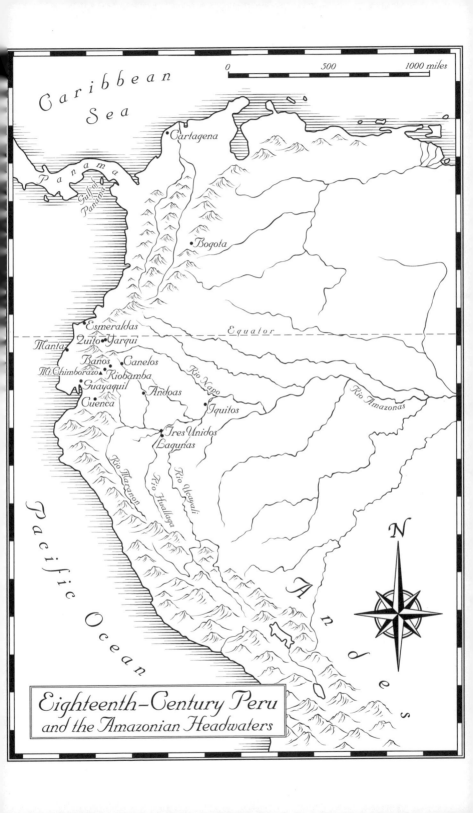

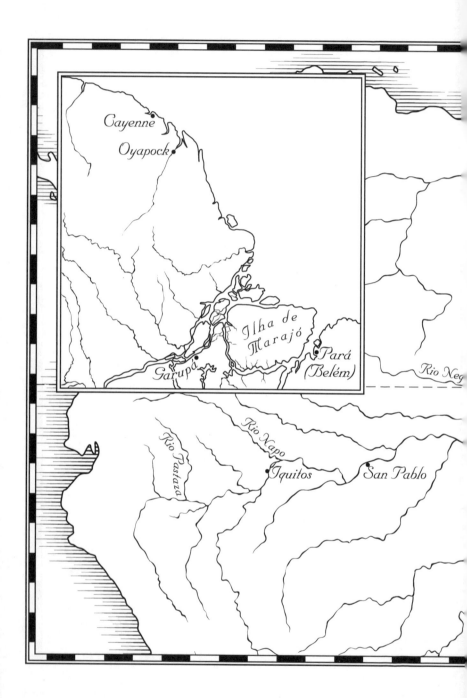

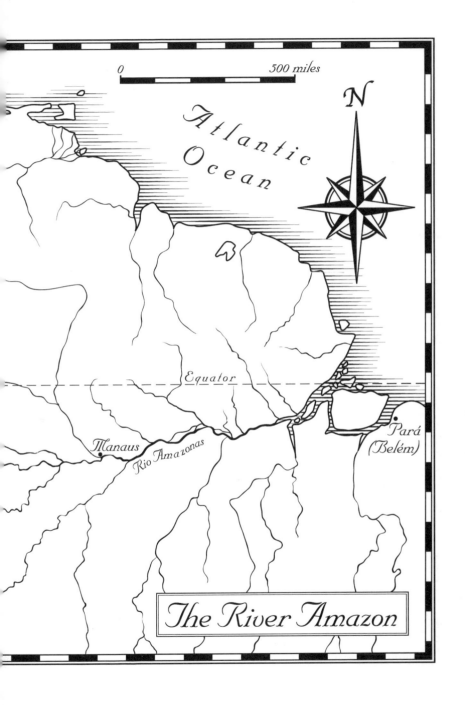

The River Amazon

THE
Lost Lady
OF THE
Amazon

A Story's Origins

The town of St Amand Montrond lies about 140 miles due south of the capital of France. It is twinned today with the town of Riobamba. This lies almost a hundred miles south of Quito, the capital of Ecuador. The connection between them lies at the very basis of this tale.

Europeans had known, certainly since 1492, that land existed on the Atlantic Ocean's other side. Its status was vague at first, and presumed to be some Asian extension, but the more it was invaded the more everyone realized that a New World lay out there; two new continents, plus scores of islands big and small. As the sixteenth century progressed so confirmation grew that a huge territory existed which, save for ancient stories from Scandinavia and elsewhere, had never been suspected. When Pedro Cabral was on his way to India he encountered a bit of it, claiming it for Portugal, but Spanish ships did most of the exploring and a Spaniard, Vasco Balboa, was first to see that an ocean lay on this New World's other side.

By no means did the Iberians then sit upon their hands. Either from greed or for adventure, the love of conquest

1

or of precious metals, they leaped at the new domain like hounds unleashed. Spain was 194,000 square miles, Portugal 34,000, and these two nations had stumbled upon a territory thirty-six times bigger than both their homelands. Despite the vastness of this colossal cake they did not content themselves with slices here and there; they wished for all of it, and as soon as possible. Within an astonishingly short time, while the rest of Europe was little more than spectator at another's feast, the Iberians occupied South America, Central America, much of the West Indies, and were pushing into North America, reaching today's California, Texas and Florida.

Their courage and fortitude were undeniable, as was their wish to take and take. The speed of their conquest was staggering, particularly when one remembers that much, if not most, of central Africa was still not known to the outside world even by the middle of the nineteenth century. In 1511 Balboa had seen the Pacific. In 1519 Ferdinand Magellan was sailing across it. In that same year Hernando Cortez was conquering Mexico, and in 1532 Francisco Pizarro was being similarly successful in Peru. If they were ruthless to those already living there they were certainly ruthless to themselves. Balboa was beheaded in 1519. Only twenty of Magellan's men, excluding himself, reached home of the 270 who had departed. Pizarro was murdered in 1541 and Cortez, the one-time 'Captain-General of New Spain', was to die a broken and neglected man back in his homeland in 1547.

By that year another Spaniard, Francisco de Orellana, had already descended the entire length of the Amazon. (Three centuries later no one even knew where the Nile originated.) It had not been Orellana's intention to do so, but he and fifty-seven others had become detached from the main expedition party. With return travel up-river then impossible, and downstream the sole alternative, they eventually reached the Atlantic, turned north-west, arrived near Trinidad, and soon sailed home to Spain. This fantastic exploit occurred less than half a century after Columbus had stumbled on Haiti.

The Iberians, so commendably quick off the mark, had no intention of yielding any of their territory. Like lions defending their kill, the Spanish and Portuguese were determined to keep everything to themselves. Way back in 1494 the Pope had pronounced how the new lands were to be divided only between Spain and Portugal with the Treaty of Tordesillas. All foreigners were to be kept at bay.

In the early days of invasion by Spanish and Portuguese the rest of Europe had not been much interested. (The rise of Protestantism had helped to keep it occupied.) Only when Spain increased her power, financed so liberally with gold and silver from her vast new empire, was there resentment. This could be assuaged, in part, by attacking the treasure ships, but the New World fortress had become, by then, too well occupied for additional invasion. There were occasional nibbles, but these were akin to jackal snatches from the lions' meat. Along the coast of northern

3

South America some Dutch, English and French gained little pieces, and each held on to them. Along the Amazon a few English, Irish and Dutch settlements were established only to be attacked and destroyed by the Portuguese. In any case there were other and easier pickings for land-hungry Europeans, now actively addressing global and imperial possibilities elsewhere. Apart from the rest of North America, which the Pilgrim Fathers would reach much later, there was Africa, and India, and quantities of the Far East either to be settled directly or to serve as trading partners before being gradually usurped. Therefore why worry about Latin America? It was already taken.

Nevertheless, for scientists it held a special allure; it seemed so exciting. Everything about the Amazon in particular demanded superlatives. It was so much bigger than every other river, and flowing through a most colossal forest which, so the stories said, was home to outlandish animals. The Andes were yet another challenge, with active and snow-capped volcanoes even in the tropics. That southern continent also had deserts where, allegedly, no rain ever fell. There were strange foods, some of which – like the potato, maize, pineapple and cacao (for chocolate) – had already been successfully transplanted. The whole region was a place demanding to be examined scientifically, to be measured, checked and catalogued. But the Spanish and Portuguese appeared uninterested in these aspects of their world. For other Europeans longing to look, and measure, and take note, the doors were firmly locked.

Suddenly, in 1735, Spain gave permission for a group from the French Académie des Sciences not only to enter, but to work and stay for a year or two. This startling shift in policy was a curious consequence of the War of the Spanish Succession, a conflict which lasted from 1701 to 1714. Philip, Duke of Anjou, a grandson of Louis XIV of France and great grandson of a former king of Spain, had succeeded to the Spanish throne in 1700. By the war's end his position was considerably more secure, and he felt indebted to France. He was therefore ready to look favourably even two decades later upon the request which arrived from the Académie des Sciences concerning a scientific dispute between Britain and France over the shape of planet Earth. The controversy, perhaps a trifling matter to some, had been hotly debated earlier that century between Isaac Newton, Britain's Astronomer Royal, and Jacques Cassini, France's Italian-born counterpart. Was the earth an elongated prolate spheroid (Cassini) or an oblate spheroid (Newton)? In other words, did our planet bulge at the equator or at its poles?

With both Newton and Cassini now dead, but the controversy still alive, French astronomers wished to send one expedition as far north as possible towards the pole and another as near as was convenient to the equator. The angles of specific stars at these two widely separated positions would settle the argument. After Spain had given its permission, however bewildered by the request, the French prepared to go north to Lapland and south to Spanish Peru.

And that, however improbable it may seem, formed a starting point for the extraordinary tale of love and separation involving Isabela Godin des Odonais and her husband Jean. For over twenty years a continent divided them. Between these two individuals, apart from South America, lay the length of the mighty Amazon, quite the most formidable of all the rivers in the world. The married couple were pawns in a much bigger game, with kings and government ministers confusingly involved, and with no one caring much any more, if at all, for oblate spheroids or the prolate kind. The pair merely wished to spend their lives together, but discovered this elementary desire to be extraordinarily difficult, due to the amalgamation of politics, and Andes, and suspicion, and Indians, and awesome Amazonia. Two decades of uncertainty had to be experienced before a couple's loyalty to each other could hope to triumph in a story which all began with that lucid, if bizarre, request from the Académie des Sciences.

CHAPTER 1

The French Measurers
1735–43

The man appointed in charge of the expedition to South America was very much an eighteenth century individual, a blend of scientist, military man and adventurer. He was a savant, an aristocratic friend of many in high places, a mathematician, an astronomer and a naturalist in an era when science was burgeoning as never before. He was, wrote one historian, 'an ensemble of all the forces of that strange age in which religion, debauchery, intellect, fashion, and brutality' were all clubbed together.

Born in 1701 into a distinguished French family, Charles-Marie de la Condamine grew up during that War of the Spanish Succession in a household frequented by generals. As a youngster he watched excitedly as soldiers marched off to war. Some of his relations would die in battles against England's Duke of Marlborough and there was occasional famine in France. As extra misery for some, a great investment crisis known as the Mississippi Bubble, left countless families destitute but, whether by skill or luck, it helped the La Condamines to become extremely wealthy. After leaving college at eighteen, Charles-Marie became an officer in the army.

He took part in the siege of Rosas, at the north-eastern tip of Spain, and there he heard from a Spanish captive of the mighty Andes and of the Inca peoples, of tropical vegetation and the quite different world that was South America. The Spaniard had planted a seed, but the allure of this other world had to remain a dream while the Spanish denied entry to all foreigners. Meanwhile La Condamine pursued his life and acquired knowledge in the broad fashion then so favoured. He studied mathematics and geodesy, astronomy and navigation, and was elected to the sixty-strong Académie des Sciences at the age of twenty-nine. He then joined an expedition to the Barbary Coast in north-west Africa, and later became a good friend of François Arouet, better known as Voltaire. This friendship blossomed when La Condamine made the writer rich. The young, and mathematically able, scientist had realized a certain official lottery was selling insufficient tickets for the offered prize. He therefore recommended that Voltaire buy the lot. The great man did so, and netted 50,000 francs.

Soon afterwards the permanent secretary of the Académie des Sciences was announcing that, with the 'generous permission of the King of Spain' and the 'gracious consent . . . of Louis XV of France, may God preserve him', two expeditions were to be despatched, one to Lapland and the other to the equator. The old, and often violent, argument between the Newtonians and the Cassinians was about to be resolved. Pierre Louis Moreau de Maupertuis, brilliant mathematician (soon to be appointed head of the Berlin Academy by Frederick the Great), would lead the northern party of Messieurs Clairault, Camus and Le Monnier. This would later be joined by Olaf Celsius, the Swedish astronomer and creator of the temperature scale bearing his name. As for the southern expedition that would have as leader, after much string-pulling, oratory and connivance by the ever-grateful Voltaire, the soldier-savant who had been so adept with the lottery. Charles-Marie de la Condamine, by then thirty-four, had also helped in his own selection by donating 100,000 livres to defray expenses, that ill-wind of the Mississippi Bubble having blown much good his way.

Whether from patriotism or expedience this expedition's leader was a professing Cassinian, holding that the planet did bulge at its poles rather than its centre. The inheritors of the old argument were still fiercely determined about the issue. When a certain Jean Richer discovered that a clock's pendulum beat more slowly at Cayenne in French Guiana than in France, thus suggesting that Newton had been right, he was strongly denounced for his 'hypocrisy' by the new Astronomer Royal, Jacques Cassini, son of the old protagonist. In the Age of Reason many people were behaving most unreasonably in this controversy and, while La Condamine probably would not have been appointed leader had he favoured Newton, one suspects he was more determined to get behind Spain's locked doors than to settle any dispute.

For all geodesists, curious about the planet's shape and its consequent effects upon gravity, the matter was important, but so much else at that time was equally intriguing. Carl von Linné (Linnaeus) had put forward his binomial system of classification that very year, giving each plant a Latin generic name coupled with a specific adjective, the system used today. Botany, as a science, was exploding, so too natural history in general, and as an exceptional all-rounder, La Condamine longed to investigate the New World. This visit to Peru was perfect. The foray suited him marvellously, and might also prove Cassini to have been correct.

It was never suggested that La Condamine and his party should travel to Cayenne in French Guiana. That colony's capital was only five degrees north of the equator, and its location could well have served to settle the argument. The Laplanders would be much further from the pole, and yet would be making measurements for comparison with those from the southern party. Therefore why did the Academy expedition not settle on Cayenne, or the Portuguese city of Pará at the Amazon's mouth, even nearer to the equator than the French possession?

The answer has to be that Peru was far more tempting. Even the difficulty of access was an extra inducement. Any Atlantic port would present less of a problem, but equatorial Peru could only be reached by travelling overland from the north of South America or across Panama and south again by ship. Then there would be the return journey, perhaps by a different route. Spain had given its permission for Peru. Therefore why debate further about an offer never previously granted to any foreigner?

And why restrict the expedition's work solely to investigating the planet's shape? Why not make it broader based? Make its team bigger than the Lapland party, which would surely hasten back from its chilling climate as fast as possible. In fact, let it consist of eleven people, including an astronomer, a mathematician, a draughtsman, a doctor, an instrument-maker, a botanist, a naval officer, a couple of assistants, and of course the administratively competent, military polymath who would be leader of them all. When addressing the Academicians before his departure, La Condamine said that 'we have been singularly honoured' by the King of Spain. Indeed they had, and they were singularly delighted to take advantage of the sudden generosity.

The Bourbon king, Philip V, may have felt secure enough upon the Spanish throne, but he did have opponents. His subjects had not much approved when, following Philip's enthronement, Louis XIV of France had trumpeted: 'Henceforth the Pyrenees no longer exist.' The Spanish were aware of increasing attacks upon their colonies, and upon the realm itself. As for the Council of the Indies, the extremely powerful guardians of Spain's western empire, its members were appalled that the king had let a group of Frenchmen in behind the door they themselves had kept so well sealed for two and a half

11

centuries. Why let in any foreigners, and particularly a group wishing to investigate? The king's word was law but, as a compromise to placate the Council, it was agreed that two captains of the Spanish navy would accompany the expedition and report fully upon all its activities.

'Gentlemen, everything is now in readiness,' reported La Condamine when concluding his farewell address to the Academy: 'Our instruments have been sent to the port at La Rochelle, from which point it is our intention to embark.' The date was 1735, and a French frigate, the *Portefaix*, had been commissioned as transport.

Those who embarked on 15 May, expecting a couple of years' absence, could not have imagined the mixed fortunes they were to experience. For some the final return to France was to be many years thence. Certainly Jean Godin des Odonais, lynchpin of this book, could not have suspected that his adventures, his frustrations and loyal perseverance in his marriage would form the talk of every salon when news came back home of his experiences. He was twenty-three years old when he set sail, and had joined the expedition in the humble role of chain-bearer and signal-positioner through the recommendation of his cousin, the mathematician-astronomer, Louis Godin who was also of the party.

Apart from La Condamine, Jean Godin and his cousin Louis, the party included Dr Jean Senièrgues, Captain Verguin of the French Navy, the instrument-maker Monsieur Hugot, the draughtsman Monsieur de Morainville, the astronomer Pierre Bouguer, the botanist Joseph de Jussieu, his assistant Monsieur Mabillon, and Monsieur Couplet, a nephew of the Academy's treasurer. From an outsider's viewpoint, with the expedition's focus on mathematics and astronomy, it did seem to be a geodesic party, specifically interested in the earth's shape. On closer inspection, the South American expedition was plainly wishing to investigate as much as possible of the land itself. No botanist, for example, went to Lapland, and that northern party was led by a mathematician rather than an all-round savant such as La Condamine, so eager to discover, to measure and take note of everything he might encounter.

The northern party reached its measuring site in the summer of 1736, and returned home to Paris with the relevant information eighteen months after its departure. Nothing for the southern group was quite so speedy. For us today the passage of eighteenth century time is hard to absorb, and it is particularly difficult to imagine that Peruvian expedition. Six months passed before it even arrived at Cartagena, the first New World port it encountered. A further six would elapse before it could hope to reach Quito, the proposed base of operations. At Cartagena the two Spanish naval officers, Jorge Juan y Santacilla and Antonio de Ulloa, joined the party, as previously agreed. The two men proved to be quite the reverse of the heavy-handed officials expected. Instead they welcomed their change in circumstance and were soon making light of the problems thrown up by that foetid, disease-laden and piratical region.

At Cartagena (in modern Colombia) the Frenchmen discovered that Quito's location was even more awkward than they had realized. It could be reached most directly by travelling 400 miles up the nearby Magdalena river before transferring everything and everyone on to mules and crossing formidable Andean mountains to reach Bogotá, 8,660 feet above sea level. The visitors would then have to proceed on yet higher mountain tracks for a further 500 miles. Monsieur Hugot, in charge of the delicate instruments, doubted if these would be in good shape after such a journey, and recommended the alternative route which involved sailing a further 230 miles with the frigate to the Panamanian anchorage of Portobelo. Crossing the isthmus from the Atlantic to the Pacific by a combination of canoes and mules brought them to Panama City, the community founded in 1515 and set ablaze by Henry Morgan in 1670. That whole region still seethed with brigandage. There was also unbridled commerce, great wealth, extreme poverty, and much merchandise rarely seen in European markets, such as Jesuits' bark (or quinine), vicuña wool, cinnamon, gold, silver and emerald, all in lavish abundance. Panama City formed a pulsing artery through which flowed much of Spain's affluence, and it was magic in the eyes of La Condamine, everything so novel, so astonishing, and precisely what he desired. However, even after reaching Panama, he and his party were still a long way from their Quito destination.

A ship, the *San Cristobal*, had been promised 'soon', though the South American length of time was difficult to gauge. De Ulloa, far from restricting the Frenchmen to geodesy, recommended proper scientific use of the delay. One group therefore charted the Bay of Panama and another collected plants. Their leader took note wherever he looked, at the 'thin waistcoats' of the women, at their near-perpetual relaxation in hammocks, at their readiness to smoke. He also wrote to the Academy in Paris that the two years it had proposed for his expedition would be hopelessly inadequate. He and his group were still far from Quito, and 1736 had already arrived. Eventually so did the *San Cristobal*, and the scientists sailed from Panama on 22 February, nine months after their departure from France the previous May.

Another three months were to pass before the French contingent reached Quito. On the voyage south from Panama La Condamine, impatient to reach land, chose to stop off at Manta, while the others went on to Guayaquil. (Both these places, including the capital Quito, are now in Ecuador, which split off from Peru during the revolutionary disturbances of the early nineteenth century.) La Condamine, as might be expected, had selected the harder route, and was rewarded by the lunar eclipse of 26 March seen above great droves of boobies and pelicans. He saw stars never observed from the northern hemisphere, and brand new kinds of people (some 'coloured red from head to toe') and a strange stretching cloth the natives called caoutchouc, formed from the sap of a certain tree. When Howard Carter was first peering into Tutankhamun's tomb he was asked what he could see. 'Things, wonderful things,' was his reply. Charles-Marie de la Condamine was seeing wonderful things wherever he looked, and took steady note, and measured; and he was overjoyed.

Pedro Vicente Maldonado, prominent citizen of Quito, governor of Esmeraldas province, and as much mathematician, naturalist and observer as La Condamine, had heard of the new arrival and hastened to pay his respects. This slightly younger man spoke Spanish, French and Quechua, the local native tongue, and the two took to each other instantly.

The party reassembled and reached Quito, the old city built at 9,350 feet, captured by the Incas in 1470, conquered by the Spanish in 1534, and made an Audiencia – a central seat of government – by Philip II of Spain in 1563. Every Quito citizen, or so it seemed, had turned out on that first day to welcome the French 'measurers'. Bells were rung, flags were waved, some Indians danced, pipes were played, and there had not been such excitement since the first European woman had arrived almost two centuries earlier. A welcoming party, led by the Audiencia's president, immediately offered the foreigners apartments in the Palacio. The hospitality was intense, and startling. All gates to Spain's overseas dominions had been locked for over 244 years, but at their very first opening, however much it displeased the Council of the Indies, the people of Quito turned the event into a triumphant celebration.

At that time one third of the city's population was Indian, one third cholo (mixed blood), one sixth

Spaniard, and one sixth negro. The Indians were little more than slaves, with the wealth of others often assessed by the numbers of Indians they owned. Spaniards of rank behaved much as their compatriots back home in Spain. As for cholos and negroes their status could be distinguished by their style of clothing and its colour, and all ranked higher than Indians, the former keepers of this land. No one else was ever treated with the indignities accorded to the wretched Indians. Quito's cathedrals, its palace, and the fine living – for some – had all been imposed upon the squalid misery of its earlier inhabitants.

The city's welcoming festivals lasted for three days. Then, though the locals still failed to comprehend why such a bunch of learned individuals should have travelled quite so far to make some measurements, it was time for work to begin. Pedro Maldonado, now as much a part of the expedition as any of them, was apparently unconcerned about his governorship of Esmeraldas. It was he who suggested Yarqui, some twelve miles from Quito, as a convenient spot for him and the foreign savants to start their work upon determining the earth's shape.

Unfortunately, the Academy treasurer's nephew fell ill. His sickness, diagnosed as malaria, caused Dr Senièrgues to pursue the contemporary fondness for blood-letting. (Cures then actively promoted could often be more damaging than the sicknesses, with a common rectal complaint then treated in Peru by a pessary of lemon, pepper and gunpowder.) Poor Couplet could not survive the lethal combination of disease plus treatment, and succumbed on 17 September – only sixteen months after leaving Paris. As De Ulloa phrased it, having observed the distemper's speediness, this victim 'had only two days to prepare for his passage into eternity; but we had the satisfaction to see he performed his part with exemplary devotion.' It was, added De Ulloa, the 'death of a person in the flower of his age [which] was the more alarming'. As for La Condamine, who had promised to take great care of the treasurer's relation, he felt uncomfortably guilty about this early and first major mishap of the expedition.

The leader's diaries at this time make no particular mention of Jean Godin, later hero of the tale. The man was unskilled, and not within the upper hierarchy. He presumably did his job effectively, helping with his mea-suring-chains to determine the distances between one point and another, but he was not involved with the mathematics. He was just one of the party which, boosted by Maldonado and shrunk by Couplet, now laboured at its task.

A first necessity was to map the land. Only then could triangulation points be fixed, crucial precursors to assessing the roundness of the earth. The region was mountainous – making one wonder yet again that low-lying Cayenne had not been chosen – and the work took considerable time. The desert area became searingly hot by day and freezing cold each night. One of the Indian helpers died. Louis Godin, mathematician, became ill.

Pierre Bouguer, astronomer, and inclined that way from the start, grew increasingly cantankerous. The instrument-maker, Hugot, worried that his Parisian chilblains had returned. In short it cannot have been much fun, either for La Condamine or Maldonado, as they too suffered in the cold and heat. At least Jean Godin was never indicted for complaining.

More disturbing for the man in charge were the Spanish grumblings. The locals became increasingly suspicious, as well they might with a group of foreigners measuring, digging, surveying, and using instruments whose purposes were quite unknown. The torments experienced by the busy French only added to the distrust. There must be some more comprehensible goal than solving an alleged controversy about the planet's shape. Finding precious ore, perhaps? And why this region of Peru? Why the specific area around Yarqui? And why such diligence in difficult places when life within Quito would be so much more pleasant? A new administrator of the region, fatter and more mentally bigoted than most, sent spies to watch the work. He questioned the servants. He caused interruptions and soon became intolerable. There was nothing for it, in La Condamine's aggravated opinion, but for him and one of the Spanish officers to travel to Lima. The Viceroy, highest administrator in the land, could then officially confirm consent for the expedition's work and thereby end the bickering.

This was no casual decision. Lima lay a thousand miles to the south, with nothing but a major portion of the

Andean mountain chain between it and Quito. Such a journey would occupy many months, and deliberations at the destination would surely consume more time. On the other hand, bearing in mind La Condamine's *curiosité ardente* (Voltaire's description), he would be seeing more of Peru and escaping his difficult compatriots. After an eight-month absence, the two men returned in July 1737 with a document to quell the big and bigoted individual who had, so providentially, given excuse for further inspection of Peru.

It was now twenty-six months since the party had left France, and the triangulation points, from which to measure star angles, were still not yet in place. The measurers had marked out their five-mile line on which the triangles would be based to span a distance of 200 miles. Their work was either excessively *ardente*, seeking out all information however irrelevant to star angles, or it was forthrightly diligent on behalf of the controversy. (The northern party was nothing like so determined in their brief summer season of work.) La Condamine could not resist examining everything, whether this team labour related directly to the main task in hand or not. They inspected the volcanic peaks, so excitingly tall, and also collected plants. They examined the variations in the dip of their magnetic needle, the speed of sound in that thinner atmosphere, and the swing of a pendulum in those different latitudes. Not every scientist notices phenomena in other disciplines but, for a polymath like La Condamine, it was all irresistible. He might have been on another planet than in this New World, so incongruous and so distinct from the one he knew.

Miserable news then arrived from the Academy. The Lapland party, led by Monsier de Maupertuis, had not only returned but was able to confirm, by comparing measurements achieved near Paris with those made in the north, that Newton had been right. The planet was indeed an oblate spheroid, as the Englishman had claimed. Voltaire, always ready to welcome the puncturing of authority, was overjoyed. 'They have flattened the earth as well as the Cassinis,' he exulted. La Condamine was devastated. Not only had his party been wrong, but all his work with triangulations had been proved unnecessary. Yet more inconveniently, and partly as a result of this unhappy news, his team started to disintegrate. Louis Godin, the mathematical cousin of Jean, was offered employment at a Lima university. The instrument technician, Hugot, perhaps not wanting further travel with his precious equipment (or wishing to avoid more chilblains), not only married in Quito, but decided to stay there. Other members of the group, knowing the principal purpose of their expedition had been removed, merely and understandably wanted to go home. By now, in June 1739, over four years had passed since they had taken their leave of France. Only La Condamine wanted the work to continue and managed to hold his team together a little longer, but soon he surely wished he had not done so.

Jean Sènièrgues, the doctor, had been giving free treatment to those who sought advice. In particular he had befriended the Quesada family in the town of Cuenca. Their handsome daughter, Manuela, had been engaged to a certain Diego de León who had then changed his mind and had chosen to marry another. The doctor was incensed and therefore intervened. He suggested force-fully to Diego that Manuela should be paid money for his breach of promise, since her chances of marriage were now much reduced, but the doctor's suggestion was not welcomed. He and Diego were therefore at loggerheads, and happened to meet in a narrow street. Jean Senièrgues, perhaps better with scalpels than with swords, drew his weapon, lunged at Diego, and missed. Worse still, he then fell over, causing the whole reputation of the earth-measurers to descend. There was yet greater misfortune at Cuenca during a bull-fight when the doctor was further provoked. Once again he drew his sword, but this time everyone became his enemy. La Condamine and the others rushed to his defence, but he was stoned and stabbed to death before they could reach him. The surviving Frenchmen were quickly given refuge in a monastery.

No sooner had the doctor died, with La Condamine fervently demanding justice from the authorities, than Joseph de Jussieu went off his head. For five years he had been collecting plants, carefully drying, sorting and packing them, but then a servant carelessly destroyed the lot. As one historian of the expedition wrote, the poor man 'never fully reclaimed the use of his senses in his life-time'. Soon there was yet additional unhappiness. In a conflict, curiously called the War of Jenkins' Ear, the Pacific coast of South America was suddenly in danger from a British fleet. (Robert Jenkins, a sea captain attempting to trade in South America, had had one ear cut off by the Spanish. They threatened to do the same to Britain's king, thus precipitating a nine years' war.) La Condamine's two Spanish captains, so helpful in quelling local antagonism, were abruptly ordered to Lima in order to help with coastal defence.

A second conflict, known locally as the War of the Pyramids, then caused even greater trouble. The Academy had suggested, even before the expedition's departure, that its base line, wherever this had to be drawn, should have its eventual positions marked by 'monuments of a permanent nature'. La Condamine did as he had been told, and erected little pyramids in the Spanish territory. This was careless, and made yet more so by decorating them with the fleur-de-lis, France's royal arms. The names of La Condamine, Bouguer and Godin were also inscribed, as principal measurers, but not a single Spanish name, not even that of Philip V. The two naval captains, now returned from their naval duties, were aghast. All of Quito was aghast. The time had long since passed when the foreigners had been welcomed with dancing, bells and flags.

La Condamine was summoned to attend Quito's Fiscal, a powerful government department. He did not respond gracefully or diplomatically, much to the fury of his host country. He explained that Philip V was himself a

Bourbon, with both Spain and France thereby linked. He argued his case, wrote to Paris for support, attended court on numerous occasions, and watched 1741 merge into 1742 with this issue paramount. In time he accepted compromise, and offered to put both Spanish captains' names on the pyramids, even above those of the three Frenchmen. This was a miserable and acrimonious ending to an expedition that had started off so well.

One bright spot in the gloom was an announcement by the chain-bearer, Jean Godin des Odonais, former citizen of St Amand Montrond, of his impending marriage. He was thirty, she thirteen, and her name was Isabela de Grandmaison y Bruno. She lived in Riobamba, about a hundred miles south of Quito and slightly to the north of the massive volcanic peak of Chimborazo. Her paternal line was French in origin, but had been naturalized in Spain before being transplanted to Peru. Her father, generally referred to as Don Pedro, was first an officer in the Spanish army. He had then travelled to South America, and there became an administrator. He was a man of means, quite apart from his wife's wealth, she being described as 'graceful, charming, and extremely rich'. Their daughter Isabela, born in 1728, was also attractive and fluent in Spanish, French and Quechua. Her education, unlike her future husband's, had been intense, although her languages had been most readily acquired by living in a community where all three were widely spoken. As an extra she had learned Quipus, the Inca method of conveying information by coloured strings and knots. Her marriage to Jean Godin would take place, most prestigiously, at Quito rather than the small village of Guzmán, not far from Riobamba, where she lived. Her family had property in that area, notably the huge hacienda of Sudtrepeid. At the ceremony Isabela arrived on her father's arm, and Jean was supported by his expedition leader.

As La Condamine looked about him during the ceremony on 27 December 1741, he must have reflected upon the mixed fortunes of his expedition. Senièrgues and Couplet were dead. Beyond repair were Jussieu, the botanist, and Mabillon who had also become deranged. Louis Godin, Jean's cousin, had taken employment at Lima. Therefore only five of his ten original companions were in good shape and among the congregation when Jean Godin affirmed his wish to marry Isabela and live with her in Riobamba. Captain Verguin and Pierre Bouguer were about to go back home, having selected the landward route via Bogotá. The wedding was undoubtedly celebrating a union, but disunity must also have been in La Condamine's thoughts that day.

Most wretchedly there was another departure shortly afterwards. Monsieur de Morainville, the expedition's draughtsman, had been helping with the construction of a nearby church when its scaffolding gave way and he fell to the ground. With that collapse La Condamine no longer had an expedition, its members now summed up as three dead, two mad, two married, two returned, one locally employed, and himself. Like some officer in a fearsome war he no longer had command, there being no member of his regiment remaining.

The two Spanish naval captains, after serving so assiduously as members of the expedition, also went their separate ways. Antonio de Ulloa, the more enterprising of the two, had been nineteen at the expedition's start and chose, following its conclusion, to return to Spain down the west coast of South America and Cape Horn. His ship was captured by the British, and he was delivered to Governor Bradford of Boston, Massachusetts, who transferred him to London where his notes and papers were returned to him as a result of intercession by Britain's Royal Society. He then travelled to Spain and with his expedition colleague, Jorge Juan, jointly wrote a most impressive book, later translated into English as *A Voyage to South America*. De Ulloa also wrote *Noticias Secretas de América*, as originally commanded. This proved to be so frank, containing all manner of unwelcome information about Spain's colonies, that the Crown dared not publish it. Its manuscript lay hidden for a century until, intriguingly, the British acquired a copy and printed it in 1826. Its author finished life as a lieutenant-general. He was elected to all the famous academies of Europe, and became the first governor of Louisiana in 1766. Its sizeable portion west of the Mississippi had become a Spanish possession in 1762, only to be returned to France in 1800 and then sold to the United States in 1803. De Ulloa died in 1795 at the age of seventy-nine.

As for La Condamine's wretched pyramids, the cause of such furore, they were to succumb much earlier. In 1742, shortly after Jean Godin's wedding and de Morainville's death, Quito's Audiencia had formally announced its decision. The monuments could remain, but the fleur-de-lis would have to go and the two Spanish names, those of Antonio de Ulloa and Jorge Juan y Santacilla, were to be placed above the three French names. This conclusion, reached only after many months of deliberation, was soon to be of no avail. When the Council of the Indies, still smarting at the original invitation to the French Academy, heard of the monuments they were mightily displeased. Therefore, six years after the pyramids' construction, they were totally destroyed, but their story still had more years to run. In 1836, six years after Ecuador had become an independent nation, the new authorities affirmed a change in policy. They ordered the pyramids to be rebuilt on exactly the original sites, but with different wording: 'The French Academicians . . . erected these pyramids in November 1736 . . . they were destroyed by command of the King of Spain . . . and rebuilt 100 years later . . . by order of his Excellency Vicente Rocafuerte, President of the Republic.'

Meanwhile, La Condamine needed a new mission to keep him in South America, and he happened to see a map of the Amazon which had been drawn by a Jesuit, Father Samuel Fritz, during his four decades of living on the river. As one Spanish captive at the siege of Rosas had served La Condamine so well as his first inspiration for

South America, so Father Fritz's exciting map of Amazonia planted the next seed. Why not travel down the mighty river, and return to France that way?

A Spaniard, Francisco de Orellana, had made the journey in 1542. Why should not a Frenchman follow in his wake exactly 200 years later? Orellana's venture, so ably chronicled by an attendant friar, had apparently only encountered hazard, with warlike Indians, food shortages, and near-permanent uncertainty whether the inland sea, as they called it, would ever reach an ocean. There was never any mention of the botany, the fauna, the natural excitements to be found along the way. Those earliest explorers had concentrated, quite understandably, solely upon survival, and did not make a proper map. Two centuries later, a savant-adventurer could be infinitely more revealing. La Condamine's equatorial expedition had disintegrated, leaving him in charge solely of himself. The river was beckoning, all 3,000 miles of it.

Pedro Vicente Maldonado, who had already seriously neglected his governorship of Esmeraldas to support the measurers, was a kindred spirit who could also not resist the river challenge. Jean Godin, although married, made a gentle suggestion that he might become a third man on the trip, but Isabela was now pregnant, and his place was by her side. Therefore he stayed, and watched his chief depart. That year was 1743, meaning that eight had passed since he and the others had boarded the frigate back in La Rochelle. Jean's circumstances had greatly changed and he was torn between wishing to accompany his leader, wanting to be in France again, and knowing where his duty lay. In a year or two that longing for his native land might overcome his local obligations but, for the time being, he waved his chief goodbye and settled down to live his life in Riobamba.

CHAPTER 2

Iberians Among the Amazons
1542, 1560–1, 1637–9

Francisco de Orellana, the first European to travel the length of the Amazon, most definitely did not have this enterprise as his original intention in 1542. He probably did not even know beforehand about the river's existence and, in any case, was not the initial leader of his expedition. That man was Gonzalo Pizarro, a younger brother of the conqueror of the Incas. He was then Quito's governor but, as might be expected of a conquistador, was unhappy with his mundane lot as administrator. Early in 1541, less than eight years after Atahualpa and his Inca regiments had been defeated, this younger Pizarro planned a further invasion of new territory. It was not so much an exploration as a foray to discover further riches. Gold had been reported east of the Andes, and so had cinnamon. Gonzalo intended to find as much as possible of both, or anything else of value which might come his way.

31

This expedition was no trifling undertaking. About 200 Spaniards were involved and almost as many horses, thus forming a greater number of both men and beasts than his brother had used when conquering Peru. There were also hundreds of pack animals, mostly llamas, as well as 2,000 pigs, and almost as many dogs, so adept in hunting Indians. Four thousand captured Indians brought up the rear who would serve, once unshackled, in any capacity for which they might be useful. The sight was assuredly impressive when this entourage of animals and men, some 10,000 in all, departed from Quito at the end of February 1541, a year when much of Europe was so differently occupied. (Henry VIII, for example, was busily divorcing his fourth wife, the protestant 'Flemish mare', and was courting number five.)

Orellana was not initially of that massive assembly departing from Quito, as he only belatedly heard of the expedition. He was then thirty years old, and had reached the New World as a boy of sixteen. He had distinguished himself in the subjugation of Peru, notably in battles at Lima, Trujillo and Cuzco. His gain in reputation, wealth and power had been offset by the loss of one eye during the fighting. Orellana caught up with Pizarro at Zumaco, some 110 miles from Quito. By then there had already been trouble, with over a hundred Indians dying from cold, the forest being difficult, and bridges having to be built over all the rivers. 'Anyone but Gonzalo Pizarro,' wrote a chronicler, 'would then have abandon'd such an enterprise, it so opposed by Heaven and Earth'. Before long 'a few' Spaniards had also died, along with 'many' more Indians.

Anyone but Gonzalo Pizarro would also have learned that torturing local people was not the soundest method of extracting truth. Wisely they always urged him on, further to the east, where gold was in abundance, or so they said. Orellana, now second-in-command, suggested restraint, but Pizarro's habit of treating inhabitants was too entrenched for change. Fighting all the while, torturing captives, plundering food, and eating much of its supplies, Pizarro's expedition was soon in terrible straits. When it reached a point 256 miles from Quito 'most' of the Indians had died, 'most' of the horses had perished, 'all' of the pigs had been consumed, quite 'a few' of the dogs, and a 'large number' of Spaniards were sick, perhaps about to join those already dead. By Christmas 1541 no gold had been found, only a few cinnamon trees, and the food situation had become desperate.

It was therefore time for desperate measures. The two leaders, Pizarro and Orellana, decided that the junior man should travel down-river to forage for food. Some captured Indians had mentioned 'extremely wealthy' tribes further to the east. Orellana should travel to meet them, together with fifty-seven men in a 'barquentine' which the expedition had constructed, and with an assortment of canoes purloined along the way. The former proud expedition, of 10,000 animals and men, which had departed so arrogantly from Quito ten months earlier, now pinned its hopes upon a single water-borne party which might, or might not, encounter food, and might then be able to return with sufficient provender to feed those left behind.

The stream this food-collecting contingent had selected was exceptionally fast-flowing. The first day of travel on its surface was successfully accomplished, but on the second the barquentine hit a tree-trunk, damaged a plank, and had to be repaired. The friar recording this foray expressed dismay even from the outset. 'On account of the heavy current' it might be impossible to return upstream. Travel overland 'was out of the question', and the men were already 'eating hides, straps, and the soles of shoes cooked with certain herbs'. This veneer of civilization is attractive, with soles plus herbs considered superior to soles alone, but there was nothing civilized about their first arrival at an Indian village. The Spaniards made a mass attack, the inhabitants retreated, and the invaders plundered food, with each man taking his fill. This sustenance, whatever it was, must have been a welcome change from chewing at fragrant boots and belts.

Then, as a major difference to Pizarro, Orellana attempted to speak with the Indians. He 'took away their fear', gave them 'some supplies', and was rewarded with 'meats, partridges and turkeys'. Unfortunately none of this largesse could serve the expedition's original purpose, with Orellana's band now 700 miles downstream from Pizarro's men. Reaching that place of bounty had been exceptionally difficult. Returning from it, and upstream as against down, was judged impossible. Orellana knew he would be damned as guilty by Pizarro, but also knew there was nothing he could do save continue downstream, and wonder what might transpire. He had no idea what perils lay ahead of them, but there was no other option. He only knew they would perish if attempting to return. The recording friar, who realized that others would read this testimony critically if it survived, wrote that the Spaniards 'did not wish to be put by Orellana into a position where they would be compelled to mutiny'. In other words they would obey their leader, but only if he pursued the single feasibility, namely to proceed downstream and forget about Gonzalo Pizarro.

To help them do so they promptly built a bigger and better boat, which they called a brigantine, with high sides as protection against arrows. Nine days after its launching they reached the main body of the Amazon river, having (probably) been on the Rio Coca until that time. From then on, as they journeyed down the greatest of all rivers, there was a certain sameness to most days. They fought Indians. They captured or were offered food, with their crossbows and arquebuses seeing much service. Meanwhile they travelled on and on, and wondered if the huge river, so infinitely bigger than any watercourse they had ever met, would reach an open sea, or end in a massive waterfall, or a lake, or even vanish underground. Portuguese sailors had been passing its huge mouth for some forty years, but it is not known how much Orellana and his men were aware of their discoveries. Certainly no one of that time knew of the possible hazards along the river's length. Their courage on this venture was quite remarkable, save that they had no other option. Downstream was the only course to take, whatever might occur.

At one point, not much to their amazement as they had encountered female warriors in Central America before reaching Peru, they were attacked by women who were: 'very white and tall . . . very robust and go about naked, with their privy parts covered, with their bows and arrows in their hands, and doing as much fighting as ten Indian men . . . [and] our brigantine soon resembled a porcupine.' The warrior women elicited no more astonishment from the friar, and presumably Orellana and his men, than the four fine-haired, white-skinned, well-mannered, and splendidly dressed 'giants' they also encountered on another day. In fact the tall males were better remembered, and considered of greater interest, being 'decked out in gold' and loaded with great offerings of food. The recording friar called the females Amazons, just as these men were labelled giants. Amazons were an accepted part of western literary tradition. In classical legend such warlike women had lived north of the Black Sea. Hercules had visited them on one of his labours. Exceptionally tall people were called giants, and female soldiers were Amazons; that was the style.

In time to come the friar's leader would rue those words so casually inscribed, as he wanted his discovery to be known as the Rio Orellana. For a while that wish was granted. A Spanish map of 1587 indicates the 'Rio de Oregliana', but this eponymous fame did not last.

The world, after reading of those women, increasingly disregarded the explorer's wishes. The story of the fighting females lasted long after Orellana died. Consequently his river is now the Amazon, save in the upper sections where Rio Solimões or Marañón – Sea or Not – is its name.

On 26 August 1542 Francisco de Orellana and his men reached the Amazon's mouth and the Mar del Norte, as that part of the Atlantic was then known. They had done extraordinarily well, losing only three of their number from Indian attack, along with the eleven who had died from lack of food before any nourishment had been found. As the friar recorded: 'We had no pilot, nor compass, nor navigator's chart of any sort, and we did not even know in what direction we ought to head.' The *Victoria* and the *San Pedro*, as the two main vessels were then known, turned left, hugging the shore past the Guiana coast to reach the Gulf of Paria which separates present day Venezuela from Trinidad, after only seventeen days, and finally encountered Cubagua by the island of Margarita from where they travelled home to Spain.

Neither Orellana nor Pizarro fared well in the few years left to each of them. The same month which saw Orellana's boats reach the Atlantic also witnessed Gonzalo Pizarro's arrival back in Quito. After realising that Orellana had 'deserted' him Gonzalo and his survivors had stolen more canoes, had occasionally found food, and had opted to go back rather than follow the second-in-command. In

August 1542 he and eighty emaciated men limped in to Quito, without a single horse, or pig, or dog, or Indian from the massive contingent which had set forth with such arrogant determination eighteen months earlier.

In Quito the disgruntled and resentful Gonzalo Pizarro learned that his brother, Francisco, the 'Marquis' and conqueror of Peru, had been murdered in June 1541 by a rival faction. Gonzalo sought revenge, with fighting and rebellion in his blood as much as in his brother's. Very soon he even killed the Viceroy before declaring himself the King of Peru. His subsequent reign was brutal. It led to the execution of 340 Spaniards, and eventually he too was executed on 10 April 1548, having lost a crucial battle against the Spanish king's replacement representative.

As for Francisco Orellana, the alleged deserter, his life was even shorter. On reaching Spain he suggested that his country should become interested in New Andalucia, as he had named the Amazon basin, and was permitted to leave on a further expedition. Unfortunately, he had encountered opposition during the planning and his trip was therefore poorly funded, but a fleet – of sorts – under his command did set sail in May 1545. This reached the Amazon, but was dogged by ill-fortune, with disease and hunger paramount. Orellana himself died, aged thirty-five, sometime during November 1546, partly from illness but mainly, it is said, from grief after losing so many of his men. The conquistadors may have killed many of those they encountered in their brand new world, but they also tended to die themselves long before achieving a normal span.

Premature demise certainly applied to the second attempt upon the Amazon, which occurred almost twenty years after the first. Orellana's well-recorded journey promised little to attract successors. He had done well, but against repeated assault from belligerent Indians. No sooner had he escaped from one kingdom, furious at his invasion, than he had met another with equal determination to defend its territory. Save for those giants decked in gold, there had been little mention of riches along the river. Therefore why should anyone bother with such a warlike and unprofitable area when there were so many more valuable and simpler pickings elsewhere?

This logic did not deter Pedro de Ursúa and Lope de Aguirre who departed from Lima in 1559 and set sail upon the upper Amazon in 1560. De Ursúa had done well in pacifying the region around Bogotá, and the Viceroy of Peru had given him command of an expedition to search for El Dorado, the Gilded One, the golden individual whose existence was perpetually promoted and generally believed. Unfortunately, among those he selected to assist him, there was Lope de Aguirre. This former tomb-robber, mutineer, horse-breaker, and one-time military man had frequently sought great riches with no success. Worse, he had once been strapped to a mule's back and publicly humiliated, receiving a hundred lashes for his maltreatment of Indian porters. Maimed for life by this punishment, he vowed revenge on the sentencing magistrate, and achieved it almost four years later when he pinioned the man to a table with his poniard. On the run for two years thereafter, often disguised as a negro, he received bullets in his leg and hand in Indian wars. As a companion to be valued and trusted on a difficult expedition he surely scored zero, or possibly rather less.

Pedro de Ursúa, described as gentle, generous and sweetly disposed, also chose to take his lady-love on the expedition. This was as wrong-headed a decision as accepting Aguirre as travelling companion. She was a certain ingredient for discontent among his 300-strong assembly not so partnered on the voyage. Even before it commenced there was trouble. Some money had to be extracted from a priest at gun-point, and four men were executed for killing de Ursúa's second-in-command. There was also food shortage, and even starvation, before the expedition was properly under way, since it set sail in boats too small for all the horses and provisions which had been planned. Gentle Ursúa and his Doña Inez were seemingly unaffected by all this mayhem, busily enjoying each other's company.

Mutiny was not long in coming, with Aguirre in charge of it. (As mutiny, bloodshed and grievance had occupied so much, if not most, of his earlier life this fact can hardly be astonishing.) He planned it for 1 January 1561, wishing to start a new year with a brand new leadership. De Ursúa had been warned of the attack, but had posted no extra guards. 'What seek you here at this hour?' he asked casually when a group assaulted him and stabbed him fatally, yelling in traditional style: 'The tyrant is now dead; long live freedom.' That leader, 'of middle size, well proportioned . . . courteous, affable . . . fond of his soldiers, and more inclined to mercy than to justice,' as the expedition's friar phrased it, thus perished at the age of 35.

His death was not the expedition's last, not by a very long way. Aguirre, as veteran mutineer, knew the next important task was to slaughter all close associates of the former commander. There is expertise in running a mutiny. As in everything else, a great difficulty lies in knowing where to stop, to cease being suspicious of possible rivals, to halt the killing. There is also a problem in curtailing ambition. Aguirre hit upon the scheme of conquering Peru. Francisco Pizarro had done it when subjugating the powerful Incas. Gonzalo Pizarro had also done it – briefly, following his separation from Orellana. In each case small, but determined, forces had achieved success. Therefore why should not Aguirre, now head of a triumphant mutiny, be similarly successful with the contingent at his command?

His plan was simple. Stop voyaging down the Amazon. Forget about the stories of a Gilded One. Think instead of the certain riches within Peru. Reach that territory by travelling north to the island of Margarita. Kill the king's representatives at that important outpost. Do the same at Nombre de Dios on the isthmus of Panama. Acquire ships on the Pacific side and sail for Peru, just as the most famous conquistador of all had done, so brilliantly, twenty-nine years earlier. But Aguirre's grand design foundered on mutiny, butchery, and finally a government ambush which led to the death of the would-be new conqueror of Peru.

To be a conquistador was to possess extraordinary courage, to be ruthless beyond belief, and almost certainly to die long before old age. Lope de Aguirre's claim to fame concerning the Amazon lay in being second after Orellana to travel down a part of it. No other Spaniard wished to follow in his wake, and none did so for three-quarters of a century. By then the conquistadors had yielded to settlers, to administrators, and to missionaries. The age of Orellana, of Pizarro, de Ursúa, and Aguirre receded into history, and a new time had arrived.

In 1637 a canoe arrived at Fort Presépio (later Pará, and now Belém) at the mouth of the Amazon, containing two Spanish friars and six Spanish soldiers. This caused consternation among the Portuguese who saw the river as a Portuguese highway into the interior. Spain and Portugal were not enemies, and even shared royalty, but were two separate nations, and kept an eye on each other. So what was taking place upstream? The Spaniard arrivals were questioned, and also entertained hospitably. They explained that their mission station on the Rio Napo, near the eastern Andes, had been abandoned owing to resentment from the local people. Most of its incumbents had then returned to Quito, but two of the Franciscan brothers had chosen to travel downstream mainly, it would seem, out of curiosity. One of the friars, Andrés, was promptly despatched by the Portuguese to Lisbon so that the authorities at home could learn of this Spanish adventure. Simultaneously the Portuguese prepared a massive expedition to travel upstream. This would discover quite what was happening in the river's upper reaches, and would be departing exactly ninety-five years after Orellana, a Spaniard, had been first to travel down it, claiming the river for Spain. Since that time, following the Portuguese encroachments, its ownership had shifted. So what was happening to the west, and how far had the Spanish invaded this river? To settle these questions the Portuguese had every wish to be first to travel up its length, no less formidable an undertaking than the single canoe's downstream voyage which had created such speculation.

The departing flotilla consisted of forty-seven canoes with seventy Portuguese soldiers, to be powered upstream by 1,200 Indians and negroes. Also on board were guns, ammunition, bows, arrows, food and items for barter with the Indians encountered on the way. In charge was Captain Pedro de Teixeira, a man with considerable experience in fighting foreign settlements up the Amazon. He and his Portuguese superiors had no wish to relinquish any of the region which they had cleared of foreign rivals. Hence the colossal expedition to make this point rather more emphatically. Spanish invasion, even as modestly as eight men in one canoe, should never be permitted. Their next such foray could well be very much larger, with perhaps as great a force as the Portuguese were now despatching.

Whereas food had not been a problem for the eight-man contingent it became hugely important for the armada of 1,280 individuals. Even so it managed to reach the first Spanish settlement on the Amazon after only eight months of paddling. Teixeira then divided his force, leaving most of it behind and proceeding onward with eight canoes. For a time this small fleet could make use of the tributary it had selected, but proceeding by foot then became obligatory. After almost a year of travel the Portuguese reached Quito. Just as the authorities at Fort Presépio had been dismayed when eight Spaniards had suddenly arrived, so the Spaniards in Quito were equally concerned when a group of Portuguese reached their city. Did this mean that Portugal intended taking over Spanish territory? If not what did it mean? And what was happening on the Amazon?

At Quito the fellow Iberians were treated most hospitably, as had happened at Fort Presépio, but there was whispering behind their backs, as speeches, banquets, ceremonies, fireworks and bull-fights kept the Portuguese happily detained without imprisonment. It was soon decided that Teixeira and his men should be permitted and encouraged to return, but with a Spanish delegation as companions. Just as the Portuguese had taken note of Spanish settlements along the river, so would the Spanish learn about Portuguese incursion.

That downstream journey took place in 1639, but it produced no great flurry of follow-up journeys either up or down the Amazon. There was little reason for anyone to travel the river's entire length merely to reach the other end. There were plenty of opportunities for Portuguese lower down the river to make a home, occupy a piece of land, and trap nearby Indians for slaves. Similarly the Spaniards moving eastwards from the Andes put down roots, occupied their pieces of land and stayed put.

So when Charles-Marie de la Condamine abandoned Peru in July 1743 with his friend Pedro Vicente Maldonado on a private downstream voyage of scientific exploration they were doing something quite original.

CHAPTER 3

A Feast of Science

1743–4

Neither La Condamine nor Maldonado were individuals to stress difficulties when there were excitements to describe. Even so there must have been hazards on occasion, not least during the trip's early stages. At the outset they had to cross and recross rivers, sway over suspension bridges held together with twisted vegetation, and be permanently drenched in rain. La Condamine's precious papers, containing all his records from those seven laborious years, were frequently dunked in water when the mules were forced to swim. There were also whirlpools of great power, such as the one below the pass of Cumbinama. These gyrating currents do not suck travellers deep into a vortex but make it difficult, especially for those travelling by raft, to escape their grip. It can be impossible for paddlers, circling round and round, to reach the safer water beyond the maelstrom which is ensnaring them. Only if lianas are thrown, and caught, and then held tightly, can the captives be pulled free. With turbulent water so frequently a danger, it was bizarre that a sudden lack of it could be yet another form of difficulty. One overnight drop in water-level left La Condamine's craft pinioned and suspended in mid-air.

When the world of 18,000-foot peaks and cloud and rain was safely behind them, the explorers encountered an important Jesuit station at Lagunas. Its missionaries provided them with two canoes, each forty-four feet long and fashioned from a single tree. Passengers would sit in the rear beneath a palm-frond canopy, well behind the engine-room of paddling Indians in the front section. For the two scientists, who departed from this Lagunas settlement on 23 July 1743, the new form of travel was surely a kind of heaven – no transport problems, no political confusion, no bickering colleagues, and nothing to be accomplished save observe, record, experience and map. Downstream other conveniently positioned Jesuits would continue to provide every necessity at each staging post. They knew more than anyone about their domain, were firmly in control of it, and of major benefit to all travellers such as the scientific pair. Quite how the paddling Indians would return to their various places of origin is nowhere mentioned in La Condamine's extensive diaries.

What is mentioned, most excitedly, is the scientific feast these men encountered. They were fascinated by the Indian procedure for stunning fish, and collected the plant from which the insecticide barbasco is derived. This possesses the alkaloid rotenone, an important ingredient of many modern insect killers. Every such revelation was new to science, as were details of the black resin with which the Indians tipped their arrows so very lethally. Having encountered this curare, collected from the bark of an otherwise harmless liana (later named as *Strychnos toxifera*), La Condamine became intrigued how this deadly substance could be used to collect most of the game they ate without making them ill. It also caused no trouble, reported the Indians, for humans wounded by the arrows, provided antidotes – such as salt and sugar – were speedily applied. La Condamine therefore shot a chicken with a curare arrow, administered sugar to the wound, and was delighted when the animal 'exhibited no sign of the least inconvenience'. (He was not always so successful when trying this experiment later on in France, but there were still occasions when 'the fowl did not show any sign of being out of order'.)

On meeting the Rio Negro, the only one of Orellana's tributary namings to survive into the eighteenth century (and beyond), La Condamine learned of a river connection between the Amazonian watershed and that of the Orinoco, lying to the north. Normally river catchment areas are separate and distinct from each other, but a major and natural stream was alleged to link the two great waterways of northern South America. La Condamine believed what he had heard, but geographers back home refused to countenance it – until forced to do so when the Prussian explorer, Alexander von Humboldt, actually travelled upon its water early in the nineteenth century.

On board his canoe La Condamine was already transporting some cinchona seeds from the red bark tree (*Cascarilla roja*), from which quinine is extracted, the beneficial medicine for malaria. The word comes from the Quecha language where *kina* means bark. The Indians knew of the tree's merits before the Spaniards' arrival, and in 1630 a corregidor of Loja apparently benefited from its use. A more famous story originated in 1638 when the Countess of Chinchón, the Peruvian Viceroy's wife, took the drug and allegedly regained her health. The tree was thenceforth known as the cinchona, but the story is confusing partly because the original Quecha word is so similar to the countess's name. At all events the Jesuits then attempted to monopolize the trade in *kina*/cinchona, and called it Jesuit's bark. La Condamine first met the substance when exploring Panama, and Europe was soon to learn of *los polvos de la condesa*, the Countess's powders. After the French explorer had brought back some seeds Linnaeus named their genus Cinchona even though the Amazon traveller had published a description of the species as Quinquina condamine, but Linnaeus – so crucial in identification – had his way. In the 1860s seeds and seedlings of the tree were enthusiastically stolen from South America by Clements Markham and Richard Spruce, British explorers, and quinine soon became of great benefit to those parts of the British empire where malaria was rife.

During his downstream voyage, and later in Paris, La Condamine was yet more fascinated by the rubber tree.

He had first observed this species in the Peruvian lowlands of Esmeraldas, but was now meeting its smooth bark at every twist and turn of the Amazon. The Indians used its latex widely, as he later wrote in *A Voyage Through the Inner Parts of South America*, published in London in 1747.

> When it is fresh, they work it with moulds into what shape they please, and it is impenetrable by the rain; but what renders it the most remarkable is its great elasticity. They make bottles thereof which it is not easy to break; boots, and hollow bowls which may be squeez'd flat, and when no longer under restraint recover their first form.

Later on, some Portuguese in Pará described other uses Omagua Indians had for this latex. That tribe had given Orellana a particularly hard time during his voyaging through their area, firing countless arrows in his direction, and provided no occasion for him to learn of a somewhat flippant use for this strange material.

> [The Omaguas] make squirts or syringes thereof, that have no need of a piston, or sucker; they are made hollow, in the form of a pear, when scoop'd, having a little hole at the small end to which a pipe of the same size is fitted; they are then filled with water, and by squeezing them, they have the same effect as a common squirt. This machine is mightily

51

in vogue . . . when they meet together by themselves for any merry-making, the master of the house never fails to present one to each of his guests; and the use of the squirt with them is always the prelude to their most solemn feasts.

Orellana would have been astounded had he known that the warlike Omaguas played such pranks upon each other; all he knew was their enthusiasm for attacking him and his boats. La Condamine, such a different individual in such a different age, and not an Omagua target, chose to make use of this novel substance, moulding it to protect his precious paperwork, gathering as many facts as possible about the tree, later known as *Hevea brasiliensis* and, later still, as a source of crucial raw material.

He diligently gathered seeds, along with the rubber itself, and took everything back to France, but the world was initially not much interested in this substance's strange qualities. Even the scientifically inquisitive Benjamin Franklin poured scorn upon a material which was only good, in his opinion, for erasing pencil marks. He would no doubt have been yet more disdainful when some later manufacturers used it to create raincoats which, melting in summertime and cracking every winter, were not wholly satisfactory. Everything had to wait until Charles Goodyear discovered vulcanisation in 1839, thus making the substance infinitely more amenable and providing it with a tremendous commercial future. As for growing the rubber tree in places distant from the Amazon, that all had to wait until 1873 when Henry Alexander Wickham removed thousands of seedlings from around Santarém in a gently clandestine manner, took them back to Liverpool, organized a special train from there to London's Kew Gardens, and eventually received a knighthood for greatly profiting the British Empire via its rubber industry, most notably in Malaya. His name is not much favoured by most Brazilians.

Strangely, during the century when there was considerable talk, and a great deal of writing, about the concept of what Rousseau was soon to call the 'noble savage', La Condamine was unimpressed by the Amazonian Indians and their lifestyle, despite his fascination with their knowledge and practical use of certain substances. Initially, and understandably, he wrote that it would be impossible to 'give an exact idea of the Americans . . . [because] one would have almost as many descriptions as there are nations among them'. Later, 'recognising in all of them the same fundamentals of character', he is happy to generalize.

> Insensibility is the basis. I cannot decide whether it should be honoured with the name apathy, or debased with that of stupidity. It doubtless arises from the small range of ideas, which do not extend beyond their needs.

There should perhaps have been argument that a people, so frequently enslaved, so subjugated by their conquerors, and then so spiritually amended by missionaries, might have been shorn of their nobility along the way. Imperialists of the following century, administering peoples equally bereft, used similar descriptions about their charges, and it is odd to learn of parallels between them and the ever inquisitive, and generally sensitive, travelling scientist of the French Academy. He never hid his opinion, and continued to express it even after meeting tribes skilled in agriculture, whose warehouses bulged with attractive food.

> They are all gluttons to the point of voracity, when they have something with which to satisfy it; but sober when obliged by necessity to be so – they can do without anything and appear to want nothing . . . Enemies of work, indifferent to all motives of glory, honour or gratitude. Solely concerned with the immediate object and always influenced by it; without care for the future; incapable of foresight or reflection . . . They spend their lives without thinking, and grow old without emerging from childhood, of which they retain all the defects.

Seven years after La Condamine's voyage Jean-Jacques Rousseau lighted on the expression 'noble savage', first coined by John Dryden, and then exploited by Rousseau in his scourge of civilization. La Condamine continued to consider all Indians 'pusillanimous poltroons to excess, unless transported by drunkenness'. Orellana would have had a yet different point of view, being so violently attacked, witnessing such courage, and surviving only because of his superior weaponry, his crossbows, arquebuses, and defensive armour. He would never have called those river Indians poltroons of any kind.

When Francisco de Orellana had travelled down the Amazon he never had more than a slight idea of his geographical position, and when, if ever, he might debouch into the Atlantic. La Condamine, two centuries later, did have that capacity. He calculated, for example, that a particular tributary's encounter with the Amazon occurred at a point four hours and forty-five minutes behind the time in Paris. This site was therefore 71°25' west of the Parisian meridian. La Condamine was making his observations with 'a good watch' when timepieces were imperfect, particularly those which had been subjected to several years of South American experience. It was therefore remarkable that he erred in his calculations only by fourteen minutes and twenty seconds, or 3°35' of longitude. As none of the Jesuits had ever attempted to define a single location along the river, La Condamine was at least making a stab, if incorrectly, at doing so. The river map he drew, and continued to draw as he proceeded downstream, was the first and best of its kind. He was not explorer, opening up new areas, but was an undoubted pioneer in measuring and observing and taking note.

He and Maldonado had left the mission station of Lagunas on 23 July. They reached Pará near the Amazon's mouth, this port now known as Belém, on 19 September, having travelled almost 3,000 miles during that time. Admittedly, with the Amazon's flow being some four to six knots, a floating log could have been as speedy, but both men had frequently stepped ashore, had made detours, had corrected the Jesuit information, had spoken with the local people (however indolent or infantile), and had still travelled an average of forty-five miles per day.

On his way La Condamine had also enquired about the Amazons, the warrior women Orellana's friar had so casually described, but found no evidence of such a matriarchal society, despite assertions that one existed 'further north' and 'far from here'. The citizens of Pará, who knew nothing of warlike females along the river, were uninterested and more curious about La Condamine's estimate of their latitude. They had always considered they lived exactly on the equator, but the foreign savant then disillusioned them. The true figure, in his opinion, was 1°28' south, much to Pará's displeasure. The scientists then escaped to investigate Marajó, the Switzerland-sized island at the river's mouth, discovering it to be a single entity. They also learned that a Carmelite missionary in that region had practised inoculation against smallpox during an epidemic, with none of his patients, allegedly, then succumbing to the virus. (This was long before vaccination was ever tried in Europe, and also long after Lady Mary Wortley Montagu, the British ambassador's wife, had famously written about a form of it used successfully in Turkey. The disease of smallpox was to play a hideous role in the Godin story after he came down the river.)

The two scientists who had started from Peru reached Cayenne on 23 February 1744 after making frequent observations along the Atlantic coast. At the French colony both men examined manatees, planted their chinchona seeds, visited the spot where Jean Richer had worked with pendulums (which should, by proving that Newton was right, have made the whole Andean venture quite unnecessary), and eventually left the colony in July, believing correctly they might find transport to Europe more swiftly from neighbouring Dutch Guiana. Their Dutch ship was twice attacked while en route to Europe, once by the British and once by the French, before it reached Amsterdam satisfactorily in November. Permission from the Dutch to travel south to France was slow in coming, preventing La Condamine and Maldonado from reaching Paris until the following February. It was therefore ten years short of three months before the expedition's leader returned home, he and his party having been despatched on what had been expected would be a two-year enterprise. By then the old furore about the planet's spheroidal shape was quite as dead as its two original protagonists, and most people had forgotten why the French expedition had travelled to Peru in the first place.

However, there remained one member of the original expedition who still wished to return to France, and in Riobamba the married chain-bearer had been wondering when and how he might achieve this. Jean Godin des Odonais was now a man with a wife and two young children. His responsibilities clearly weighed on him. News of his father's death eight years earlier had at last filtered through to Peru. There was now property in his name and family matters to arrange in France. It was high time for him to go back home. After all, he had been abroad for fifteen years. There was rumour too that he had fathered a child by a young widow 'of the highest nobility related to the Viceroy'. Whether this tale was true or not, the gossip provided another reason for starting afresh in France. While in Riobamba he had continued to engage in some scientific reconnoitering, intriguingly describing 'planting signals on the highest mountains'. He also made the hard overland journey to Cartagena on the north coast, allegedly for 'business reasons', and while there maybe explored the possibility of taking passage for France with his family. Cartagena had, after all, been the French expedition's first port of call all those years ago, and Bouguer and Verguin had managed to sail for home from there. But the Spanish and the French, while not exactly at war, were never entirely amicable and on this occasion the Spanish must have been unaccommodating because Godin seems to have discarded Cartagena from his reckoning and now turned his attention to the Amazon.

All the news reaching Peru from La Condamine and Maldonado had been promising. There was no hint among their reports of major difficulty. Riverside mission-aries had arranged transport and had performed all that was necessary to assist the voyagers. Godin's personal visit to Cartagena had proved difficult and uncomfortable. Therefore a trip down the Amazon seemed the best means of getting home, provided it was satisfactory for a wife and family. However, it would be unwise for them to venture upon those waters until he, Jean Godin, had tested the route's general suitability for such an enterprise. Isabela was pregnant with their third child when he set off on their behalf to reconnoitre the river Amazon. His plan was straightforward. He would travel down the river, reach Cayenne, arrange some sort of return passage to France, and then travel upstream to collect his wife and children. The idea was audacious and novel, but seemed entirely sensible. What other way was more convenient than voyaging along the greatest river in the world?

CHAPTER 4

The Constant Husband
1749–65

Jean Godin, who had left Riobamba and his family in March 1749, did not reach Cayenne until April 1750. Therefore, although he never made measurements or major detours, as his more scientific predecessors had done, his journey had taken him slightly longer. It is possible that the Spanish and Portuguese mission stations along the river were less enthusiastic to assist one low ranking individual, but Jean affirmed he had been 'received in all the Portuguese establishments, the missionaries and fortress commanders, with all possible affability'.

At San Pablo (today's São Paulo de Olivença), the first major Brazilian community to be encountered east of Peruvian Iquitos, Jean Godin had acquired a 'small boat'. Most of the world's great rivers take downward leaps every now and then, such as the Zambesi at the Victoria Falls, such as the Nile with all its cataracts, and such as the Congo which is impassable to ocean-going traffic within a couple of hundred miles of its gaping mouth.

Even the Amazon's twin river, the Orinoco, also fed from the Andes, abounds with rock-strewn spillways along its length, making travel by this river quite impossible over major distances. The Amazon is not like this. In fact the gradient of this greatest of all rivers is so slight that at Manaus, a thousand miles upstream from the Atlantic, the bed of the Amazon is actually below sea-level. So Jean Godin did not experience too much difficulty in steering his modest vessel downstream at roughly six knots to the port of Garupá.

He had then intended to go directly, via the Amazon delta's northern branch, to Cayenne, but had to wait for permission from the Governor of 'Grand Pará'. Monsieur François Mendoza Gorjad was so effusive in his 'kind reply' that Jean decided to meet him and pay his respects. This meant 'going the long way round', and departing through the Amazon's delta via its southern arm. The governor received Jean Godin 'with open arms, put me up, would not allow me to eat at any table but his own, insisted that I stayed for eight days, and did not want me to go until he himself left for Saint-Louis de Marañao where he was going to do his rounds'. The governor's generous hospitality did not end at that point. Jean was escorted back to Garupá with a bigger boat, and there he found an even larger vessel waiting for him on the governor's instruction, captained by a 'Sergeant of the Garrison'. Powered by fourteen oarsmen it then took the French chain-bearer right up the coast to Cayenne. He therefore arrived in style.

Having reached the colony of Guiana, one of the first things Jean Godin did was write to his former leader in France to report his achievements and outline his immediate plans: 'Anyone but you, sir, might be surprised that I had undertaken a journey of 1,500 leagues so off-handedly, only to prepare another, but you are aware that travels in South America demand fewer trappings than in Europe.' As for the family journey, it would, he asserted be 'the most convenient form of travel for a woman, sparing her a long voyage by land in a mountainous country where mules are the only vehicles'. In his own passage downriver he had collected a few plants, notably the medicinal sarsaparilla, and he sent these off to George-Louis Buffon, the French naturalist at the Jardin du Roi, but he certainly did not possess the ardent curiosity, or energy, or enthusiasm and drive, of La Condamine. The fact that his journey occurred two whole centuries after the exploratory expeditions of Orellana and Aguirre might make it appear as if Amazon travel was by then a commonplace event, but long-distance Amazonian voyaging was rarely undertaken. Spanish missionaries and other forms of settler tended to approach the river from the Peruvian headwaters, while their Portuguese equivalents went upstream from the river's mouth. Hardly anyone travelled the length of it, as Jean Godin had done. In effect, he had been the first tourist, travelling solely for personal reasons. He had simply used the Amazon as a non-equine, non-mountainous and distinctly preferable means for getting halfway back to France.

Nevertheless, having come down, he then had to go up. After writing to La Condamine he subsequently wrote to Monsieur Rouillé, minister of the French Navy, asking for assistance in the matter of a passport. In his opinion the authorities in Lisbon, very much in charge of Brazilian territory, should be officially informed of his wish 'to ascend the Amazon for the purpose of proceeding to my family, and bringing it back with me by the same channel'. This request, in Jean's view, was entirely straightforward. In the eyes of almost everyone else it was so politically fraught that it was presumed impossible to achieve. One Frenchman of no particular position and importance was asking for permission to proceed for many months, and also for many hundreds of miles, through a Portuguese colonial possession and then through many more miles of Spanish colonial territory merely to be reunited with his wife and children. Then, having regained their company, he wished to bring all of them, for a similar number of miles and months, back through the same territories.

That old Iberian desire to keep the Americas free from foreigners had not gone away merely because one scientific team had once been temporarily admitted. So far as the authorities were concerned that single laissez-passer for the Academy's measurers had been concluded. The Frenchmen had entered, had been tolerated, and had done their work. Then, those of them wishing or able to do so, had departed, with the last one leaving their domain in 1749. The doors had been opened, and then most positively shut. The earlier permission had been granted by none other than the King of Spain. The French party had been despatched under the auspices of the Académie des Sciences, also royal in its status, and the Spanish Viceroy in Lima, the king's personal representative, had commanded the Quito Audiencia to accede to that team's wishes. All of this unparalleled and royal exemption had ended with the expedition's termination. It was true that Jean had married a Spanish woman, a creole within a Spanish dominion, but he himself had been born a Frenchman. His ready acceptance by the Cayenne authorities had confirmed that point. The man had become a Frenchman all over again, and was wishing that his family should also become French. Therefore, despite his marriage and the lengthy residence in Peru, he had once more become a foreigner, having lost his Spanish rights.

At some point Jean Godin must have realized the hopelessness of his situation. Correspondence with his Peruvian family was well nigh impossible. Catching a ship from the French colony to Peru was yet more so. Even La Condamine and Maldonado had failed to book passage home from Cayenne. In any case every journey on the high seas was fraught, whether undertaken with ample money, good authority, or nothing of the kind. Those were difficult days for all forms of journeying, whether on the ocean or overland. The whole of a continent existed between Jean and Riobamba. And several thousand miles of river. The former chain-bearer might as well have been on the moon for easy access to his family, or so he may have presumed during his darker hours. He was certainly an unwilling resident of French Guiana, being penniless, powerless, and on one side of South America while his family was on the other.

One thought which Jean never seems to have contemplated was desertion. It would have been easy for him to abandon his marriage and smuggle himself aboard some ship heading for France. Isabela's family had money, she would not have starved. But although Jean's situation in Cayenne was without much hope, the option of desertion never surfaced. He and his family were a unit, and would stay that way.

He continued to write letters to La Condamine and officialdom, but without any detectable advancement of his cause. In a forthright and intemperate manner he also suggested in his correspondence that France should be more vigorous about South America. He wrote in 1750 that it should enter the timber business with him as crucial middleman. In 1751 he again agitated for state funding, and the following year did receive some governmental cash from the 'Master of Ceremonies'. In 1754, with this financial assistance, he built a boat, hoping to return with it to Pará, and then demand a laissez-passer personally, but he never made the trip. (Or rather he reached the Amazon's mouth, but went no further, blaming the boat's condition for his withdrawal but possibly apprehensive about the form of welcome he might receive. Would he be arrested or tolerated, and then permitted to travel upstream? Either increasing wisdom or decreasing bravado helped to turn him round.) In the following year, after a request from Cayenne's governor, he was chasing some runaway slaves, but it is not recorded if he caught them. To help his funds he was officially granted a concession for manatee farming, with the raising of these lethargic beasts for meat, which La Condamine read in yet another letter, optimistically expected to 'rebuild his fortune'. As he had arrived in penury it is unclear which fortune he had in mind.

He did receive information from Peru, via La Condamine, that his wife's third pregnancy had been satisfactorily concluded with a daughter. That was surely welcome news, but happening 3,000 miles from Cayenne. By 1757, with the years still slipping by most casually, he started conventional farming at Oyapock, in the southeast of the colony near its frontier with Brazil. He also became involved with immigrants from Alsace-Lorraine after a plan had been initiated to settle them near Kourou, not far from Devil's Island, but the scheme did not prosper. The initial consignment of 14,000 determined individuals quickly shrank, for all manner of reasons such as death, to a few hundred three years later.

Not many of the projects in which Jean Godin was involved were ever successful. His farming venture at Oyapock became so impoverished that, after it had been running for four years, the place was producing insufficient food even to satisfy its slaves. Cayenne's governor grew increasingly unhappy with this unwilling, forever complaining, and most unwelcome citizen, eventually removing his rights to work with manatees. It is difficult to know whether Jean was truly impoverished or merely greedy for more money, but increasingly easy to sympathize with the governor. Jean Godin forever asserted that someone – France, Guiana, the Academy – owed him a living.

As the years passed by so steadfastly, with Jean no nearer his family than at the start of his Cayenne confinement, events in the bigger world had been altering, usually to the detriment of France. In 1751, one year after Jean's arrival from the Amazon, Robert Clive won a significant battle against a coalition army of French and Indian troops near Madras. The 1750s witnessed a steady reduction of French influence in that subcontinent. In 1759, on the other side of the world, the French lost their former hold upon much of Canada following the Battle of Quebec, with Britain again triumphant. As for the mighty territory of Louisiana, claimed for France and Louis XIV in 1682, the 1760s witnessed its dissolution, all the land west of the Mississippi ceded to Spain in 1762, and east of the river becoming British territory the following year.

News of the North American and Indian losses surely filtered through to French Guiana, and therefore to the one-time chain-bearer. Without doubt he was saddened by this waning influence and, seeing the world so straightforwardly through his own eyes, hit upon a plan. If losses were occurring what about a gain or two to act as recompense? He wrote to the Navy Minister that France's interests 'would be served' if it took over the Amazon's '*rive gauche*'. France was losing in the global scramble for power and ought to recoup those deficits by invading and then annexing Brazil's northern half, the left bank of its mighty river. He, Jean Godin des Odonais, loyal Frenchman and local expert, could be adviser to this occupation, having reconnoitred the Amazon but a few years earlier. Could any other Frenchman be quite so useful to such an enterprise? Could any enterprise be quite so beneficial at this difficult time in France's history?

While warming to this topic he outlined the region's commercial possibilities, having seen so much in need of exploitation during his travelling. The timber that grew in such luxuriant abundance could either be exported or lead to ship-building on a massive scale. There were various crops about which France was quite ignorant, either of their husbandry or their sales potential. The Portuguese in charge were laggardly, and most unenthusiastic about the area's development, whereas French leadership and energy could alter the situation to France's great advantage. As one final benefit of his nation's occupation of all that land there would no longer be problems about a laissez-passer for one man and his family. His difficulties would disappear, with the Godins once again united. The plan, in Jean's myopic vision, was eminently sensible – for France, for French Guiana, for restoration of former glory, and for one unfortunate couple temporarily separated by a continent and its confounded politics. He therefore detailed his scheme in an impressive 'Memoire' on the 'Navigation of the Amazon' which was despatched from Cayenne in 1763 on board *L'Aventure*, 100 tons, Captain, Louis Picard.

The letter was undoubtedly bold, but by then thirteen years had passed since Jean's arrival at Cayenne. He was no nearer his family than at the start. He had not even seen the last of his children who, if all had gone well, would be fifteen years old. What of the others and what of his wife, now in her early thirties? Jean's frustration had bubbled to the boil. With France losing Canada and India and Louisiana, it was plain that his nation could, and should, take over northern Brazil as an immediate response. The haughty Portuguese deserved such treatment, having been so unresponsive to a single individual with such a small request. They had humiliated him and, in consequence, had also humbled France. Therefore why not a retaliatory invasion, and then an occupation, to set the matter right?

Almost at once Jean Godin, as was his nature, regretted this advice, so blatantly inscribed on behalf of France. What if *L'Aventure* were intercepted when en route to Europe? The Portuguese might not be developing their Amazonian kingdom very speedily, but certainly had no wish for others to do the job. To aggravate his lonely paranoia within Guiana, and as the months passed by, no reply came back to him from France. Was this confirmation that his letter had been captured, or no more than slovenliness on the Minister's part? (Or, which never seems to have invaded Jean's mind, was the Minister a great deal saner than to trust controversial messages to naval transport? Mail-bags of foreign vessels were, when captured, often of greater interest than their other valuables on board.)

Meanwhile Charles-Marie de la Condamine, aware of Jean Godin's plight, and reminded of it by mail several times a year, continued to make all manner of intercession on his former colleague's behalf. He wrote directly to the kings of Portugal and Spain, and persuaded others in greater authority to do the same. His books on South America were well received, and he had become an authority for the entire continent. It was up to him to rescue the final and most unhappy member of his famous expedition. Again and again he put pen to paper, as avidly and almost as frequently as the unfortunate former measurer languishing in Cayenne.

La Condamine's published writings achieved their greatest renown in the scientific world and, most importantly, sparked off Spanish scientific interest in Spain's overseas dominions. Antonio Condal was sent to the Orinoco, together with Peter Loefling, a disciple of the great Linnaeus. José Celestino Mutis, although employed as physician to the Viceroy, not only initiated his own 'Expedición Botánica', but imported herbalists and artists from Europe to work with him. He eventually wrote *Flora Bogatá*, a thirteen-volume manuscript of 4,000 pages based on 105 boxes of botanical specimens and 6,840 drawings. This formidable achievement was never published, but provided further indication of Spain's abrupt and growing scientific interest in Spain's New World. This was further augmented, most crucially, by Charles III, King of Spain from 1759 to 1788. His interests were quite different from those of his predecessors, and he was forever despatching expeditions to South America and southern North America on behalf of science. La Condamine had not only opened the door, showing that foreigners could gain access. He had also shown the door-lockers, notably Spain, that the form of investigation he had pursued was thoroughly worthwhile for them.

In short, however much Jean Godin's situation had stayed static, the rest of the world had been busily altering, with a wide-ranging interest in the dormant continent finally awoken. Not only was science now leaping ahead, but former politics had shifted. Previous antagonism and suspicion between France and Spain had turned about, these two countries soon fighting as allies against Great Britain (during the Seven Years War from 1756–63). Other alliances were also being formed and it was a muddling period for all forms of nationality, with heads of state particularly bizarre in their separate origins.

In 1748, when the important Treaty of Aix-la-Chapelle was signed, the King of France was half Italian, while his heir was half Polish and married to a German. The King of Spain was French, the King of England was German, and the Empress of Austria was as much French as Austrian, her mother from Lorraine. Europe was split into two parties with little respect for the continent's geography. On France's side her allies were Spain, Portugal,

Prussia, Sweden and the two Sicilies. On Britain's side were the Austrian Empire, Holland, Russia and Sardinia. French authorities, whether civil or military, were more interested in all this European activity, and the possibility of new treaties and alliances, than was Britain. The British were happy that arch-enemy France, so closely involved with the matrix of European rivalries, could spare little time, or money, or men, for its interests overseas.

In France's capital the Court remained engrossed in its own affairs. Had Madame de Pompadour successfully banished a new mistress? What did it mean that she had been appointed lady-in-waiting to the Queen? Who was she favouring to take over this or that army, and what new friendships was she brokering? The British and Prussians were busily forming a bond on behalf of Germany, this amendment causing the balance of power to shift back and forth. Former discords were resolving, new alliances were forged.

In the midst of this turbulence the King of Portugal was suddenly experiencing a change of heart concerning letters arriving so frequently, and from such good addresses, on behalf of a certain Frenchman residing in Cayenne. France's ambassador in Lisbon was becoming most persuasive, and this new ally seemed to have a case. Perhaps the diplomat could, or should, be comforted. Perhaps it was timely, however insignificant the matter, to help one aggrieved and former member of a French scientific expedition without too much inconvenience. Perhaps some form of transport could be requested and arranged.

The date of 18 October 1765 was surely memorable for Jean Godin des Odonais. By then he had been separated from his wife for sixteen years and seven months, and had been in and around Cayenne for all that time, save for the thirteen months of travelling down the river. Jean still had no idea how he and Isabela might be reunited, and now over the horizon appeared a galiot, with thirty oarsmen under the command of a Captain de Rebello. It had come up the coast from Para and when it had anchored at Cayenne, it passed on the instructions which it carried from the King of Portugal. The captain affirmed that his vessel had been ordered to collect a Frenchman named Godin, transport him up the Amazon, wait for him to gather his wife and family, and then bring everyone back to French Guiana.

The governor at Cayenne was both delighted and astonished. At last, if all went well, he would be rid of an outstandingly difficult and perpetually demanding fellow citizen. Everything that most unwelcome resident had so frequently requested had finally come true. The waiting galiot, entirely suitable for river transport with its thirty oars, was ready for its passenger. A miracle of miracles had suddenly occurred.

As for that passenger, so frantically frustrated for so long, his reaction to the arrival was rather different. In short he was appalled. He remembered only too well his intemperate letter suggesting that France should invade and then conquer northern Brazil. This sudden arrival of a river conveyance, allegedly for him and then for his family, was too miraculous an event to be believable. It had to be some kind of trap. The captain's orders, said to be directly from the King of Portugal, added to this suspicion. A king could not possibly be personally interested in a single chain-bearer, but would be properly concerned about every form of treachery likely to damage his country. Who was this Jean Godin? Was he the prior instigator or merely the middle-man of some scheme hatched in France? The trumped up story of an abandoned wife, and of a couple's separation for almost twenty years, was scarcely convincing. Therefore this alleged unfortunate should be captured for the greater truth to be acquired. What better way than to send a boat, express sympathy for his plight, offer assistance, collect the man, bring him to Pará, and discover what villainy was afoot?

Jean's poor mind, in turmoil ever since he had sent the 'Memoire' letter, soon convinced him that his folly had been exposed. He would not compound it by walking casually on board. Their pleasure at his capture would be denied to them, those tricky Portuguese. What kind of fool did they take him for? Did they really think he would walk, so readily and calmly, into the noose they had prepared? There was only one thing he could do, and that was stay behind. Protesting some form of illness he retreated to his bed.

CHAPTER 5

A Galiot for a Lady
1765–6

Cayenne's governor was astonished. The galiot's captain was dismayed. And Jean Godin adamantly refused to cooperate, considering his bed and confinement the safest place to be. The more he considered his situation, the more disagreeable it appeared. He would have no servants with him. He would be in the company of thirty Portuguese while travelling, for the main part, through Portuguese territory. Their captain, De Rebello, had said he would accompany Jean all the way to Peru. Everything was abruptly all too good to be true. Once out of sight of French territory, and beyond French jurisdiction, the Portuguese would be in command, able to do whatever they chose with one conniving foreigner who had dared to suggest that Brazil should be invaded.

As for Cayenne's governor, Monsieur Fiedmond, there were two sound reasons for him to be incensed. The first was Godin's intransigence, but the second was this pro-longed stay by an alien vessel within his harbour. What was that captain and all his oarsmen doing, if not spying on the port's facilities? What better way to gather such information than send a vessel full of seamen, and better still to arrive equipped with an honourable purpose, purportedly acting on behalf of a stranded Frenchman? The boat's captain and the colony's governor did not meet, but communicated by letter, by increasingly acrimonious correspondence. The captain was firm, with the royal orders from his king so very explicit: pick up one Frenchman and depart with him up the Amazon. The governor saw his own position with equal clarity: get rid of the alien Portuguese as soon as possible. In peremptory fashion, after several weeks of mounting irritation, he ordered the galiot to depart with all its oarsmen, and with or without its intended passenger.

Godin then belatedly, and surprisingly, agreed to go on board. Because the Portuguese vessel was not an ocean-going craft, it would have to hug the shore when returning to the Amazon, and would therefore visit Oyapock at the eastern border of France's territory, where Godin had a house. There it did soon halt, much to the captain's swift regret because several of his rowers immediately absconded. And so, once again, did Jean Godin. He knew it was his last chance for disappearance. To his grave suspicions about the captain's intentions he had added the notion of collusion.

Why was Cayenne's governor so enthusiastic that Jean should accept the foreign offer? The governor blatantly wished to see him go. Therefore had this French official been plotting with the Portuguese? And were the two nations using him as a pawn, the better to solve some other problem? (In this Jean Godin was half correct. The governor had been attempting to improve relations with the Portuguese, and the continuing fracas with Godin had done nothing to help his friendly overtures. By delivering Godin into their hands, and by trusting the captain's word, he would be demonstrating to the Portuguese that his earlier congenial approaches had been sincere.)

From Oyapock yet another Godin letter went off to La Condamine, alleging that the boat had stopped for him to gather some belongings. Instead he was being dilatory, and hoping some happier solution would present itself. The boat's captain was in a quandary, and it is easy to sympathize with his predicament. After a long wait at Cayenne, and then eviction, he had at last been transporting his apparently reluctant passenger. Now he feared this individual might vanish once again, or take to another bed. Should he therefore capture Godin, forcibly take him up-river, and then off-load him in Peru? Or, if Godin did abscond once more, should he proceed without the husband and try to retrieve the wife? His instructions had come directly from the King of Portugal, and were absolutely clear. At Oyapock, with his anxieties increasing by the day, he grew steadily more impatient.

Jean Godin then settled the matter. This unwilling passenger reported that he had suffered a fall in the woods, and his presence on board would have to be excused. He also claimed, in another letter to La Condamine, that he had fallen dangerously ill. The illness was plainly severe, causing the boat's captain 'to wait extremely kindly for six weeks . . . Seeing finally that I was not in a fit state to embark, and fearing to abuse the patience of this officer, I begged him to continue on his way.' After a month and a half at that Oyapock outpost Captain de Rebello was first to reach his tether's end. He ordered his remaining oarsmen to their places, and headed south-east for Pará without his passenger on board. The date was 24 January 1766. In a few days he would be back at his home port. His superiors there would know what best to do.

At Pará the galiot's captain was told to stick to the original command, in so far as this could be achieved. He should proceed up-river as far as possible. If the husband refused passage that was not critical; the second portion of the royal command could still be organized. The lady could be collected.

Jean Godin meanwhile had entrusted money and a packet of letters to Tristan d'Oreasaval, described as a doctor and friar, and Godin's long-time friend. He was also, as would become apparent, a scheming opportunist, happy to take advantage of free transport up the Amazon. Godin's letters were addressed to various people along the route, to Quito's principal Jesuit, to the Superiors of all the mission stations, and also to Doña Isabela. The funds were to defray any expense the bearer might incur in delivering this mail. Tristan d'Oreasaval, 'a person in whom I had every confidence', had promised to wait at the arrival point until Isabela was on board. He would then accompany her and her party down-river to Cayenne. Jean Godin had therefore done all he could, save of course for putting himself on board.

On the face of it a mission of mercy, this journey of De Rebello's involved a secondary benefit, which the King of Portugal may well have had in mind. It would afford an opportunity to investigate Spanish invasion into Portuguese territory in the up-river province of Loreto. That extremely thinly populated region west of Iquitos was borderland, with no one knowing precisely, or even vaguely, which bits belonged to Portugal, which to Spain, and who was then in residence. The two countries were still on amiable terms, but there is nothing quite like a border dispute to upset friendliness.

In theory, according to the fifteenth-century papal Treaty of Tordesillas, Portugal was entitled only to a modest eastern portion of South America. In practice, with the Amazon beckoning settlers in the east to head further and further upstream, the Portuguese had occupied far more territory than was officially their due. The Spanish had mainly settled west of the Andes. Nevertheless, according to Tordesillas, they had been allocated territory in almost all of South America. It was a situation which the next three centuries had done nothing to clarify.

De Rebello and his thirty oarsmen, after he had gathered replacements from Pará, took eight months to reach the up-river Loreto region so rich with ownership uncertainty. As for his journey along the river, he surely and frequently felt a different form of doubt. The Amazon, despite its formidable quantity of water, is easier to navigate when travelling downstream from the Andes to the sea. (A floating cork can make the journey, and many fallen bits of tree are equally successful.) For anyone travelling in the other direction the river's tremendous width, sometimes several miles across, can make the correct course difficult to select. To row in the river's middle is to meet the fastest downward current. To row near either bank is to meet a gentler flow, but also fallen trees. Hugging the shore also creates less awareness of the river's major channel, and it is very easy to make wrong choices. It is also very possible to despair, having taken a day or two – or more – before realising one's mistake.

De Rebello and his rowers did extremely well to reach their destination in only two-thirds of a year, having departed in January and arriving sometime in August 1766. Presumably, holding the king's command, the boat's captain could exact much of what he needed by way of provisions from mission stations along the route. They would probably have had stocks of turtles, as well as dried meat or living goats still bleating discontent, and most certainly there would have been plantations of manioc, the basic starch-provider in that area. River fish were abundant, and easily caught and roasted. As for the forest itself, so dominant on both sides of the river, it is not a market stall readily suitable for passing travellers. There are occasional palms, often with nuts that are good to eat, but collection takes time, and knowledge, and it would have been easier to demand whatever had been gathered at the settlements.

Rebello and his rowers did well to journey some twelve miles every day against the river's flow to bring back one Creole family for an uncooperative Frenchman who was living near Cayenne. It cannot have been easy for De Rebello to keep them labouring at their oars for all those months, and his feat was laudable.

Tristan d'Oreasaval performed a great deal less admirably. It is not known how he spent the money entrusted to him, save that it was not used on behalf of Jean Godin. He apparently started some business ventures, either en route or at the destination, but the man 'thought fit' by Jean for 'fulfilling his purpose' was not, it would seem, even fit for fulfilling purposes of his own, since these failed one by one.

As for the precious letters they were treated with as much respect as had been accorded to the money. A 'dark-bearded missionary' is said to have received them, with promises to deliver, but he proved no less casual than Tristan d'Oreasaval had been. This man was a Father Yesquen about whom no more is heard. According to Godin, who described the whole proceedings to La Condamine, D'Oreasaval's casual behaviour 'was an unforgivable blunder, looking very much like ill-will'. Apparently considerable delight was given to all manner of people in all sorts of places as they read the correspondence. Rather more importantly, neither the Father

General in Quito, nor Isabela at her home near Riobamba saw the letters which were their due.

So how had Isabela Godin been faring since her husband had departed over seventeen years earlier? An immediate answer is that tragedy after tragedy had struck her. One by one all three of her children had died, the last to go being the girl she had been carrying when Jean left their home. Smallpox had been the killer, leaving Isabela as a middle-aged woman with neither her man nor any of their offspring. By then she had moved to Guzmán, a community much smaller than her birthplace of Riobamba. None of this was known to Jean Godin, save for news via La Condamine of his third offspring's birth. He had presumed Isabela would be living with reasonable contentment in the company of her father, various other relations, her servants, and their Indian labourers.

A description of Peru's Quito area was later provided by the two Spanish captains, Antonio de Ulloa and Jorge Juan y Santacilla, who had accompanied La Condamine's expedition from Cartagena. South America was an entirely new experience for them too. They were also young, being much like modern travellers who are excited by novelties and happy to generalize from brief experience. In their book, *A Voyage to South America*, the two men were no less critical of the Indians than La Condamine had been.

They are so indolent and slothful that, instead of working, they often loiter about the streets during the whole day . . . [They are] generally shoemakers, bricklayers, weavers, and the like . . . The most active and tractable are the barbers and pleb-otomists who . . . are equal to the most expert hands in Europe. The shoemakers, on the other hand, distinguish themselves by such supineness and sloth that very often you have no way . . . than to procure materials, seize on the Indian, and lock him up till they are finished.

The captains were a little more enthusiastic about the area's natural assets, such as the birds.

[Those] seen in this hot climate are so numerous that it is impossible to give a full idea of them; particularly of the beauty and brilliance of their various plumages. The cries and croakings of some, mixed with the warblings of others, disturb the pleasure, which would flow from the melody of the latter, and render it impossible to distinguish the different cries of the former; but are another instance of the equity observed by nature in distributing her favours; the plumage of those birds being the most beautiful, whose croakings are the most offensive; while, on the other hand, those whose appearance has nothing remarkable, excel in the sweetness of their notes . . . To describe all the extraordinary birds would result in a prolixity of little entertainment or use.

As for the major houses in that Quito area, such as the ones which Isabela occupied, they were 'spacious and well contrived', generally with a balcony towards the street.

> [Materials used] are adobes, or unburnt bricks, and clay; and to the making of the former the earth is so well adapted that they last a long time, provided they are defended from the rain. They are cemented or joined together by a certain substance called sangagua, a species of mortar of uncommon hardness, used by the ancient Indians for building houses and walls of all kinds, several remains being still to be seen near the city . . . sufficient proof of its strength and duration.

The dress of the ladies of the first rank (of which Isabela would have been a member) consists of:

> a petticoat . . . with every part of their dress covered with lace . . . Those which they wear on days of ceremony are always of the richest stuffs, with a profusion of ornaments. Their hair is generally made up in tresses . . . [with] a kind of rose at their temples. These roses are elegantly intermixed with diamonds and flowers . . . [Indian hair was] generally thick and long, which they wear loose on their shoulders . . . even when they go to sleep . . . The greatest affront possible to be offered to an Indian of either sex is to cut off their hair; for

whatever corporal punishment their masters think proper to inflict on them, they bear with a dutiful tranquility; but this is a disgrace they never forgive; and accordingly it was found necessary for the government to interpose, and limit this punishment to the most enormous crimes.

De Ulloa and Juan are not overwhelmingly sycophantic towards any section of Peruvian society, and certainly give least praise to the Mestizos who:

> do not want for audacity in any kind of theft or robbery, though in themselves arrant cowards. Their common practice is to snatch off the person's hat, and immediately seek safety in their flight . . . However trifling this may seem, yet sometimes the capture is very considerable; the hats generally worn by persons of any rank, and even by the wealthy citizens when dressed in their cloaks, are of white beaver, and of themselves worth 15 or 20 dollars . . . besides a hatband of gold or silver lace, fastened with a gold buckle set with diamonds or emeralds.

The only employment of 'persons of rank', according to the Spaniards, 'is from time to time to visit their estates, where they reside during the time of harvest'.

Very few ever apply themselves to commerce, indolently permitting that lucrative branch to be possessed entirely by the Chapitones or Europeans, who travel about the country, and pursue their interest with great assiduity . . . Some few Creoles and Mestizos so far overcome their indolent dispositions as to keep shops.

It would therefore seem as if Isabela had time on her hands, possessing personal servants and not unduly immersed in unwelcome activity. One historian, perhaps mixing imagination with fact, tells of her magnificent gardens abounding with hollyhocks and geraniums. Another states that her lifestyle was 'easy and convenient'. (And this, to leap ahead in her story, makes the events which later surrounded her all the more remarkable.) It is impossible to know with what affection Isabela Godin viewed this relaxed style of living, so disapproved of by De Ulloa and Jorge Juan, or if she had preferred hearing from her husband of the differing rules and customs operating within France. St Amand Montrond, Jean's home town, may not have represented the height of French sophistication, but he could tell her about Paris and that may have had more appeal. In any case at Riobamba he was a foreigner. He came from somewhere else and Europe, from a South American viewpoint, must have held a certain exotic fascination.

Isabela Godin may not have received any of the letters from her husband, but rumour did eventually reach her. Apparently Father Yesquen had passed the letters to another who, as Godin later expostulated, 'exonerated himself in the same way, saying he had given them to yet another'. Hearsay can sometimes travel swifter than a written message, and may be unreliable, but can give the gist of a piece of news, however casually. What Isabela seemed to be hearing, making no sense whatsoever, was that a boat had arrived on her behalf. Other rumours said there was no such boat, with doubters and believers of the story accumulating in equal numbers. In no account was there any mention of her husband, and no news that he still lived, let alone had been in the business of organising transport. The rumour therefore had to be discounted. It was simply too far-fetched.

Nevertheless it did not go away. Other stories from other sources arrived to assist with confirmation. There was some kind of boat, and it was foreign. It had been waiting quite a while, its purpose to collect the Doña Isabela, and take her down the Amazon. It was a Portuguese boat which had arrived from Cayenne. Its captain and crew were wishing to return with the Frenchman's wife. This wife from Riobamba should therefore travel to find the boat, waiting on one of the rivers leading downstream to the Amazon. The rumours persisted. The boat, with its many oarsmen, was large enough for the lady and her family, and this venture had been ordered from the highest level.

The eastern foothills of the Andes create so many streams, and the boat's crew might have reached any one of them before having to call a halt; but which one did they choose? Poor Isabela, uncertain and yet hopeful, half-believing and also disbelieving, knew the next step was up to her. As the very first item on her agenda, when still most ignorant of the alleged boat's possible whereabouts, she had first to check the story. Therefore she despatched her negro servant Joachim, a loyal member of her household, to look for it. Together with half a dozen Indians he set off to seek the truth. Only when he had returned, with news either good or bad, could she decide what next to do. It would be many months, at least, before he might come back.

CHAPTER 6

Joachim's Journey
1766–69

Joachim and his few Indians had been set quite a task. This former slave had been purchased by Isabela 'from the tyranny of bondage', as she phrased it, and he was therefore devoted to her. Working for her family, he surely knew Quito, Riobamba, Guzmán and Otavalo province (where Isabela's father was corregidor), and would be accustomed to travel among the Andes at several thousand feet above sea level. Now he had to negotiate the eastern portion of the Andean mountain chain, traversing this last colossal buttress before he could descend to scour the many tributaries for the Portuguese boat, assuming that it existed.

Everything about the Amazon is superlative, it being greatest in so much. Some of its downstream tributaries, such as the dozen which are over a thousand miles long, dwarf most rivers of other continents. The Madeira, largest of them all, is 3,000 miles from source to sea, while the Andean mountains which feed such a plethora of lesser rivers are second only to the Himalayas in scale and fierceness. With such a lofty spine running for 4,300 miles as a one-sided backbone to South America, and with so much flatness lying to its east, it follows that all the streams hurtling from this mountain range are exceedingly violent as they drop down urgently from its considerable heights to join the plains below. Worse still for passing humans, the valleys through which these mountain rivers run are often almost sheer.

What is happening, and with such hasty vehemence, is a transference of Andean material from western South America to the Atlantic in the east, with the Amazon serving as a major carrier. On the seaward side of this river's enormous mouth the silt it has already transported from west to east has formed a deposit some two miles deep on the Atlantic floor. The task of making one massive mound (beneath the waves) from the Andes (still standing tall) is continuing steadfastly, with the river's colour throughout its length a very muddy brown. People talk of moving mountains, of certain tasks impossible to achieve, but the Amazon is performing such an act, most frantically in its upper reaches, and then most stolidly for several thousand miles. In time the Andes will go completely, their material having been transported from one side of that southern continent to the other.

For most of the Amazon's length this huge river more or less parallels Earth's equator. Only in the region near the Andes does it flow from the south, with the actual source being quite a distance from Earth's central belt.

This precise starting point is disputed, there being so many possibilities, but everyone agrees it is some high point well to the south of the equator. As this diminutive and proto-Amazon proceeds northwards it steadily gathers water from countless slightly smaller tributaries. They all then join the bigger river, adding their portions to an Amazon which eventually heads eastwards as if remembering the spot where it finally finds the sea.

The tributaries lying nearest to Riobamba were those that Joachim had to search, making his way down the steepness of their valleys, drawing a blank, climbing up and over whatever lay between that region and the neighbouring tributary. Each successive failure led to the examination of yet another stream to ask about the boat. This task was formidable. It is therefore small wonder that, after several months had passed, Joachim returned to Isabela, admitting he had failed. He had been 'stopped', according to Jean, without detailing what had caused the halt. But during his absence rumours about a boat had strengthened rather than decreased. Consequently, the loyal servant was despatched once more, this time with 'new orders' and 'greater precautions'.

Joachim knew, as the rumours had related, that the boat had travelled westwards as far as possible, and as far as a rowing boat could achieve. When the particular river which Rebello had selected ceased being a navigable stream, and it had started to run too fast, he had had to call a halt. There he had moored, and had waited. The letters brought with Tristan had been distributed, and there was nothing more which he could do. He could not himself abandon his boat and search for the lady Isabela in Spanish territory; that was not part of his command. It was up to her to learn of his presence, hopefully by the letters. Then it was up to her to find her way to him.

Time, of course, was still slipping by. All in all it was now more than three years since the arrival of the Portuguese galiot in Guiana, and Jean Godin himself had been in that colony for a few months short of twenty years. One can only marvel at the single-mindedness of his determination to be reunited with his wife, and so much other commitment to helping him achieve his goal.

Just as there is no suggestion that Jean should desert his wife so is there no mention from the Peruvian quarter that Isabela might renounce a husband whose caring, but careless, wilfulness had placed him on the continent's far side. The two of them were man and wife, and that was that. Perhaps Jean knew only too well that reception in his home town of St Amand Montrond would be excessively tarnished by any abandonment. He might never be forgiven, not by the church, not by his family. As for marrying another that would be quite impossible (short of papal dispensation) unless information reached his way that Isabela was no more.

For her there could be no question of another marriage whether Jean had died or merely absconded. Middle-aged widows held little appeal, with her own marriage when aged 13 reminding her that youth was more successful. The terrible attack by the impulsive Dr Senièrgues upon the dismantler of an engagement had occurred mainly because the girl in question, accepted and then rejected, was no longer so eligible. As for Isabela, married, middle-aged, and a three-time mother, she would not re-marry; that was a certainty. Jean Godin was the same, however far removed and however helpless his situation. Even so, it is possible to wonder how many other marriages, undertaken by Europeans in distant foreign countries, were conveniently forgotten, as and when there was reason to do so – such as a parting of their ways. Jean and Isabela surely had reason, but this was never contemplated on either side. There would be no severance of their relationship until death did intervene.

The former slave named Joachim was surely illiterate. Certainly nothing has been preserved from him about his wanderings, and difficulties, and undoubted mishaps, when trying to find the boat. Therefore, as descriptive substitute, there is *A Voyage to South America*. Within their volume de Ulloa and Juan, the two Spanish captains, had much to say about the difficulties of travel within Andean territory. Their words do help to explain Joachim's predicament when, once again, he set off to find the boat. These naval authors write of rock from which water 'precipitates itself' to make a 'beautiful cascade . . . fifty toises (300 feet) in height'. All of the east Andean pathways are steep, and others so 'narrow as hardly to afford a passage for the mules'. It was dangerous to cross the streams, and doubly so to use the bridges:

> these structures, all of wood, and very long, shake in passing them; besides, their breadth is not above three feet, and without any rail; so that one false step precipitates the mule into the torrent, where it is inevitably lost.

The bridges, 'by the rotting of the wood under water . . . are annually repaired towards winter'. Accidents were 'not uncommon', mainly with the animals. These mules were, it would seem, just as aware of the perils involved in this form of travel as their masters. Whether there was a 'dreadful abyss' on one side or a 'steep eminence' on the other, they took especial care:

> The mules themselves are sensible of the caution requisite in these descents; for, coming to the top of an eminence, they stop, and having placed their fore feet close together, as in a posture of stopping themselves, they also put their hinder feet together, but a little forwards, as if going to lie down. In this attitude, having as it were taken a survey of the road they slide down with the swiftness of a meteor. All the rider has to do is to keep himself fast in the saddle without checking his beast; for the least motion is sufficient to disorder the equilibrium of the mule, in which case they both unavoidably perish.

Beforehand the mule, somewhat understandably, 'trembles and snorts at the danger'. As for the rider, doubtless trembling and snorting in similar style at the prospect of the meteor-like descent, he 'cannot fail' to be filled 'with terrible ideas'. The accompanying Indians 'go before, and place themselves along the sides of the mountain, holding by the roots of trees, to animate the beasts with shouts, till they at once start down the declivity'.

The Spanish captains, so disdainful of most humans in the area, are full of respect for these animals, being amazed:

> with what exactness they stretch out their fore-legs, that by preserving the equilibrium they may not fall on one side; yet at a proper distance make, with their body, that gentle inclination necessary to follow the several windings of the road; and, lastly, their address in stopping themselves at the end of their impetuous career. Certainly the human species themselves could not show more prudence and conduct. Some mules, after being long used to these journeys, acquire a kind of reputation for their skill and safety, and accordingly are highly valued.

Whether or not Joachim made use of such equine tobogganing is nowhere stated. It may have been the reason for his initial return, but in any case the mule behaviour paints an alarming picture of travel in the Andean foothills. Mud and trees, rivers and waterfalls, declivities and steepnesses, they all formed a part of it, and so too did the rain. All seasons were bad, according to the Spanish captains, but the beginnings of summer and winter were worst, 'the rain then causing such dreadful torrents'. The tracks themselves could be covered in water, some so damaged 'there was no possibility in passing', save by sending Indians ahead to mend them. The town Indians never received praise in the Spaniards' book, but their 'surprising dexterity' in the forests was much appreciated. They would 'run into the woods', soon return 'with branches of trees and vijahua leaves', and then 'in less than an hour' erect huts 'so well covered that the rain, which comes on very violently, does not penetrate them'.

It is only too easy to be concerned about Joachim. As a negro and one-time slave, living in times when status was so very clear, could this man demand that Indians should clear a road for him, help him cross narrow swinging bridges in visible need of repair, and put him on the backs of animals with such a terrifying procedure for voyaging downhill? Or did he have to walk, as best he could and unaided, from one valley to the next, and from one river to the next, while wearily pursuing his goal of one Portuguese vessel waiting somewhere with its oarsmen for his lady Isabela?

This vessel must, by then, have possessed an equally weary complement of individuals wondering how much longer they would have to stay, by the king's command, upon a stretch of river in the upper Amazon. They had no idea when their penance might be ended. While

Joachim was floundering, clambering, travelling, wading, and approaching ever nearer to their position, they were reaching the conclusion of four very tedious years. When would they ever see their homes and families again who existed in distant Pará?

It is therefore difficult to know which side was more delighted when the encounter eventually happened, either the black stranger who knew all about the Doña Isabela or the boatload of oarsmen, perhaps about to abandon hope for her actuality. The meeting occurred at Lagunas, the Jesuit mission from which La Condamine and Maldonado had set out on their journey. The mutual rejoicing must have been extreme, with Joachim exultant that his two-year journey had been successful, and the sailors now optimistic that their four-year vigil stood a chance of being concluded. For each of them, the finder and the found, a light had shone at the end of a very lengthy tunnel.

When the jubilation diminished, and practical thoughts began to surface, the realisation grew that nothing immediate would take place. Joachim was some 300 miles from his base, as any condor might casually spread its wings to make the journey, and it would take him quite a while to return there. Isabela would have to be informed, would have to make her plans, and all such preparation would consume more time. Nevertheless, from the boatmen's viewpoint, everything had altered. The Doña Isabela did exist. She would surely come to meet them, or send a message that she would stay in Riobamba (much as her husband had chosen to stay in Guiana). In either event the boat and its patient crew would eventually be free to travel downstream. The delay would be a matter of months, rather than weeks, before this lady could be on board, but at least it would not be years. Their wait was not yet over, but a beginning to its end had triumphantly occurred. They must have waved goodbye to Joachim with marked enthusiasm.

Meanwhile, back at Cayenne, Jean Godin remained quite ignorant of events taking place on his behalf. He still knew nothing of his family, or of his children's deaths. He certainly did not know of Joachim, a man so determinedly acting for him. He may have wondered if everything could have been hastened had he believed Rebello's story and accompanied him. Just how dangerous had been his illness, if indeed he had been ill at all? Could he not have travelled with the boat, even if lying on a sick-bed in its midst? Had he acted with excessive caution? That must have been the governor's opinion, with the unwanted Godin still around. It is easy to suspect that, while Joachim was desperately trying to find the boat, the governor and his least favourite citizen were trying to avoid each other with equal desperation.

Meanwhile three thousand miles upstream the faithful servant had returned to Riobamba. Not only did Joachim then give his mistress news of the boat, and of its whereabouts, but was also able to report that her husband was still alive but had been too ill to make the journey with the Portuguese. Or rather, as much time had passed, that he had been alive four years earlier. Now Isabela was in possession of the facts she had to come to some great decisions. What kind of a woman she had been, or had become, is nowhere clarified. One longs for a description, and Victor von Hagen, writer and traveller on South America, gives enthusiastic freedom to his pen in his *South America Called Them* (1949). He may even have been right.

> When young, Isabela de Godin . . . had been a handsome woman with deep brown eyes, an oval face, prominent cheek-bones, laughing lips that gave her face a wild-wood, voluptuous expression. Now in 1769, beyond the age of forty, her once voluptuous bosom had lost its appeal, her face, although still young, was matured by the tragedy she had suffered, as well as the strain caused by the separation of more than twenty years from her husband.

She was certainly older than Jean had been when he, with concern whether the journey might be too hazardous for a young woman and children, had set off on his journey of reconnaissance. The tables had therefore been turned wholly upside-down. It was now up to her to make the tremendous journey without even his assistance. She does not appear to have debated the issue after Joachim's return. She would go – somehow, but first had to make preparations to depart from the only place she knew, the place of her birth, of her children's births, and of her family.

Her father, Don Pedro de Grandmaison y Bruno, learned of his daughter's decision, presumably with some anxiety. Women such as Isabela did not make forays of the kind she was contemplating. Indeed few people travelled from the mid-Andean settlements around Quito and Riobamba over the mountains lying to their east. The Incas had not done so. The famous view from Machu Picchu, their ancient city north-west of Cuzco, provides a daunting spectacle of a twisting valley far beneath the amazing pinnacle. Orellana and Pizarro had found the streams and forests of the eastern Andes exceptionally difficult – even for conquistadors. So too had La Condamine and Maldonado. Joachim certainly knew about its problems. And now the Doña Isabela was proposing to go through the same difficult area, a middle-aged woman more used to living peacefully on an estate, and surrounded by sufficient servants to care for all her needs.

Don Pedro decided to help her, as his son-in-law had done, but he would stop short at the boat, knowing that the hardest section of her journey would be across the eastern half of the Andean chain. Therefore, although a score of years older than his daughter, he would check her route's suitability, make preparations with the mission stations along the way, and then see her safely settled on the galiot. So with a contingent of Indians to help him on his way, he bade his daughter farewell, promising to send word when all had been arranged. As a father he saw his duty very clearly. His Isabela and her Jean should be reunited – at long last. That was very plain, and it was up to him to do everything possible to make it all occur.

CHAPTER 7

Doña Isabela Embarks

1769

Don Pedro, Isabela's father, is a shadowy figure. There are no descriptions of him, save that he was a widower at the time of his reconnaissance. He had two sons, Antoine and Eugenio, and two daughters, Luisa and Isabela, with Isabela the oldest of the four.

As Isabela's father was also living singly he was therefore doubly sympathetic to his daughter's state. Although he could not understand why Jean had not returned to collect her, as had been the plan in 1749, he knew that travel through or even around South America was always difficult – or plain impossible – for those without considerable funding, or rank, or urgent cause. As it was, in the years thereafter, he only knew the basic fact that his daughter was solitary in Peru and her husband was also on his own so very far away. Then, with a suddenness astounding everyone – not least himself, there came the rumour and then the positive news of a boat ready to take her down the Amazon. A miracle had occurred.

Don Pedro would certainly have wondered why his son-in-law was not on board the mysteriously underexplained boat. It was so extraordinary that a group of Portuguese, neither Spanish nor French, had made the journey on behalf of a Franco-Spanish family. And how astonishing it had been to learn from Joachim that these men had been waiting, not for weeks or months, but for several years to carry out their task. Had Jean been with them he would certainly have disembarked from the boat the moment it had halted. Then he would have found his way to Riobamba, and personally brought the happy tidings to his wife a great deal earlier. There must have been a formidable reason why Jean was missing from the crew, and yet another reason, no less remarkable, why those boatmen were serving so valiantly in his stead. Joachim had mentioned a king's involvement, but kings are unconcerned with such trifles as minor citizens wishing to be united. In short there were many answers to be learned, but such questioning could wait. More importantly the boat should not be kept at anchor longer than strictly necessary.

After extracting from Joachim all the crucial information at least Don Pedro knew the boat's location. The mission station of Lagunas on the Rio Huallaga lay 300 direct miles from Riobamba, but was nearly 500 miles by the route he would have to take to reach it.

From Joachim he had learned that De Rebello had done extremely well to reach that isolated place, to row quite so near his destination, only concluding the river voyage when 27° west of Pará. To get there those men first had to travel 2,300 miles to Iquitos, the large community sited above the Amazon's union with the huge Rio Napo. Then, after rowing another sixty miles, they had to disregard the equally huge Rio Ucayali and fork right on to the similarly sized but major stream of the Rio Marañón (as the Amazon is now known in that area). After another 140 direct miles they eventually reached Tres Unidos, named for the three streams which there unite. The Lagunas mission station was situated slightly upstream on the Rio Huallaga and it therefore lay, by the waterway's meandering contortions, about 400 river miles from Iquitos. That total of 2,700 upstream miles, against an increasingly determined current, had been a formidable undertaking.

By then the stream against the rowers was just too strong, and the river too steep, making further up-country travel with such a boat quite impossible. Despite their considerable mileage from the starting point of Pará the galiot was now moored less than 500 feet above sea level, with the huge river along which they had travelled having ascended, on average, only a couple of inches in every mile. For that reason, along with the massive flow of water, the rowers had never encountered forbidding rapids along the way.

The size of Don Pedro's party is unknown, but there may have been servants as well as Indians. At Baños he arranged for a litter to be constructed. This would enable his daughter to be carried on Indian shoulders rather than experience the difficulties of walking on her own two feet. He told everyone en route of Isabela's forthcoming journey, and arranged supplies of food for her expedition. At Canelos on the Andes' eastern side, where there would have been views (above the tree tops) of the relative flatness lying ahead, he met the missionaries in charge of that settlement. They promised to do everything necessary for the woman soon to be travelling in their region, and would provide canoes and paddlers to take her safely down-river. Jivaro Indians would do this work, a tribe famous for shrinking the heads of rivals killed in battle, but who had recently been pacified and 'Christianised', said the fathers. They were therefore reliable – at least in that area, and would transport Isabela down the Rio Bobonaza to Andoas on the Rio Pastaza. Other Indians from another mission station would then take over the task of bringing Isabela and her retinue along the next leg of her journey.

At Tres Unidos on the Rio Marañón the anxious father turned south up the Rio Huallaga to reach Lagunas and the Portuguese boat crew. They had been overjoyed when Joachim had come their way. Now here was welcome evidence of further progress. Don Pedro explained that he had surveyed the route for the Doña Isabela, the palanquin had been arranged, food caches had been established, missionaries had been notified, and agreements had been confirmed about canoes and paddlers. It was now only necessary to send word back to Riobamba that all was well. The next stage was up to Isabela.

Doña Isabela Embarks

His message was brief. Everything was ready. Canoes and men had been arranged. Roads in the Andes were bad, and river travel on the eastern side would then be better, but canoe space would be extremely limited. Therefore she should keep her numbers low, and refrain from excessive baggage. As for her loving father, he would wait for her with the Portuguese at Lagunas. He may have been tired from his travels or he may simply have wanted to keep an eye on the foreign boat. There were certainly many questions he could ask about his absent son-in-law.

Meanwhile at Cayenne no news of these events were reaching Jean Godin. So much was happening on his behalf, and yet he had no inkling of any piece of it. His doubts about refusing the galiot's offer of free travel must have increased, but there was nothing he could now do to amend that earlier, and possibly erroneous, decision. He could only presume the letters entrusted to Tristan had reached their destinations, and hoped that everything was happening correctly – provided the miraculous offer of assistance from the Portuguese had been genuine. If it had been false, and the galiot had merely returned, empty-handed, to Pará his future was bleak. Therefore he had to hope he had been wrong, that the boat had proceeded to Peru, that somehow it was collecting his wife, and that she and he would meet again. The date was October 1769. He had said farewell to her on his departure from Riobamba in March 1749. Even four years had passed since he had seen the boat. So what had been happening in all that time?

For Isabela there was much to do. She had to arrange
to have prayers recited for the repose of her soul – should
misfortune overtake her. She had to decide what best to
take, and what to leave behind. There were properties to
dispose of, either by sale or gift, and she had to experience
countless sorrowful farewells, to family, to friends, to the
only world she had known. As for her party being kept
small that was a problem. Her two brothers Antoine and
Eugenio, wanted to accompany her, one because he wished
to visit Rome on behalf of his Augustinian order, and the
other had business to achieve in Spain. Also brought along
his ten-year-old son, Joaquín so that he could go to school
in France. Of course she wished to take Joachim. She also
recruited three mulatto female servants, Rosa, Elvia and
Heloise. In addition there would be thirty-one Indians, at
least for the early stages. These people knew the roads,
such as that canyon through the mountains east of Baños,
and they would help considerably. Don Pedro had not
indicated precisely what he had meant when recom-
mending that she kept her party small. Presumably she
hoped that a total of thirty-nine, including herself, was
more or less what her father had in mind.

At the last minute three Frenchmen arrived, begging to
be among her party. Their principal was described by Jean
Godin (in his lengthy letter to La Condamine describing
the whole business) as '*le Sieur R . . ., soi-disant Médecin
français*'. (His name, in fact, was Rivals, as other docu-
ments affirmed, but Jean never gave him more than a
single initial followed by the dots.) This man was therefore

either professing to be a doctor, or an alleged doctor – much like the unreliable Tristan d'Oreasaval. His companions were a valet and a negro. His previous plan, after leaving 'High Peru' (with no explanation about his reason for being in that area), had been to reach some French possession in the West Indies, such as Martinique, and then use that island as a stepping stone to France. Plainly, as he realized after hearing of the galiot, there was great advantage in travelling directly to Cayenne.

Isabela was unwelcoming, not wanting to increase the numbers in her party, but Rivals appealed with greater success to her brothers. Would it not be beneficial to have a medical man with them? How else would they circumvent disease or attend to mishap? Isabela considered she had no right to add yet more to the passenger list, but was persuaded. Her small party therefore became forty-two rather than twenty-nine, and the French were overjoyed.

So on 1 October 1769, twenty years and six months after Jean Godin had himself departed, Isabela set out from Riobamba, knowing she would be reunited, God willing, with her husband sometime in 1770. Her long wait, accompanied by so much tragedy, was coming to an end. Isabela knew that the first part of their journey through the cordillera would be the most troublesome. The ravine they would be following had a steepness, a slipperiness, and an awkwardness which was about to prove even worse than her expectations. Had Isabela read of De Ulloa's mules, snorting and trembling before their bobsleigh antics down the forest paths, she might have been better prepared mentally for what was to come. As it was, panting uphill and panting downhill, she and her party learned all about Andean travel as they made their way, slowly, uncomfortably, and most miserably, along the chosen route.

Of course it rained. It rained at night, and it rained by day. The Indian-made and makeshift shelters served reasonably for sleep, but nothing could be done about the all-pervading wetness when each day arrived. There were trees across their path, and lianas, and fallen branches. Nowhere else does botany strike back, it has been said, with as much wilfulness and spite as it does in South America. Even sedges can cut at skin as if they are formed from razor blades. Certain palm-like fronds have thorns and spikes which hold a passing human captive. It is possible in this rain forest to end up bleeding quite dramatically merely by strolling through a piece of it and brushing past its vegetation. And regretting doing so.

Isabela and her party were not strolling. They were wishing to descend several thousand feet as fast as possible, and reach the flatter environment around Canelos. In the meantime, resenting the plants which tore at them, disliking the ants and other insects so keen to take advantage, and understanding with every stride why those eastern Andes were such a barrier, the party continued on its way. If it stopped for a rest it could soon regret the halt, with ticks and various insects ready to catch a hold at every opportunity, or fallen branches ready to trip the unwary. And made yet more discomfited, and bruised, and miserable at the whole sorry business.

From Baños to Canelos is a straight forty-four miles. The Indians did their best to help those less able than themselves, such as the ten-year-old nephew, the three maidservants who were possibly making poor progress, and Isabela. She was the oldest but also the most determined. She was no more acquainted with forest travel than her three attendants but she had more drive, more purpose, and – almost certainly – less readiness to complain. Joachim would, no doubt, have been a tower of strength, knowing the way, pointing out his earlier difficulties, and glad of everything's fulfilment. As for the three newcomers, they must have been acquainted with Andean travel, and had to accept this initial price to be paid for the free and more luxuriant journeying they would experience down the Amazon. In any case they were young men, and therefore at an advantage over middle-aged Isabela. Or her nephew. Or those three maids.

At least the whole contingent was proceeding downhill, alongside the rivers. Canelos lay ahead, with calmer waters and a fleet of canoes prepared for their arrival. Voyaging by river would be definitely preferable to the cavorting, skidding, clambering chaos of stumbling within a gorge. The thought of sitting in a canoe, and of being paddled past the forest, was greatly superior to the wearisome actuality of proceeding through it. There would be proper daylight, and not the cavernous gloom of life beneath the trees. There would be movement without effort. All the steep and slippery surfaces, of mud, of fallen branches, and of mossy rocks, would be satisfactorily in their wake. Ahead of them would be a smooth and open waterway leading to the galiot, and then with that galiot to the sea. Such thinking would have been paramount in everyone's mind as Isabela's party stumbled from the high ground to low. Even the air felt different as the altitude diminished. Everything felt different as Canelos came their way. What merriment there would be on reaching this initial destination.

After nine days of forest travel, and having left the Andes positively behind them, either Joachim or the Indians would surely have been first to see the mission station, a group of thatched huts within a clearing open to the sky. It looked silent, as such places tend to look, when they approached it. The arrivals could see no one walking, either in the compound or by the river's edge, but this was not troublesome. More importantly the place was Canelos, their first and most crucial stopping point. The mountains had been vanquished. As for the river, there was still a current, but nothing like the desperate torrent there had been for several thousand feet. The turbulence could now relax and make gentler passage for almost 3,000 miles. Its river water, now so kind and easygoing, would soon be joining the colossal Amazon.

The visible lack of people at Canelos did seem extraordinary. There should have been a modest bustle, of food-preparers, of men and women going about their business, of children consuming energy. All new arrivals are intriguing, particularly those coming from the hills, but no one seemed to care as nobody was in sight.

There was only one reason for such an emptiness. Isabela's Indians were first to sense it, and made the point by vanishing. Without delay they scattered into the surrounding trees. Now Isabela's party sadly understood the reason. The single cause to have created such an instant flight, more fearful than enemies, was the terror known by many names but mainly as viruela. Isabela and her group were not the only recent visitors to Canelos; smallpox had got there first.

CHAPTER 8

Disaster

1769

Everyone knew of smallpox and its ravages. European adults had either experienced its vesicles and pustules, and had then survived with or without disfigurement, or they were still susceptible. As for South American Indians, so vulnerable to disease imported from other continents, they had become inevitable victims of the smallpox epidemics. They rightly feared its arrival in any area, knowing that flight from those already infected, and from the place of their infection, was the only course to take.

At Pará in 1745, following his journey down the Amazon, La Condamine had observed a system of inoculation used to forestall 'la petite vérole'. He had been impressed, and thereafter became a firm advocate of this form of prevention. As with so much else he was ahead of his time. Not until 1796 did Edward Jenner inject an eight-year-old boy with cowpox before giving him smallpox and then watching him survive.

Meanwhile the disease was all pervasive in South America, and it was therefore no surprise that the Canelos Indians vanished the moment they realized that someone had been afflicted, and no less certain that Isabela's Indians would also vanish from Canelos as soon as the reason for its emptiness had been understood.

Jean Godin suggests, in his telling of this portion of the tale to La Condamine, that the Andean Indians in Isabela's party may even have been frightened by the river and its canoes, being quite unaccustomed to such travel. 'It is not necessary to look for good reasons for their desertion; you know, Sir, how many times they have abandoned us on our mountains, without any rationale, during the course of our operations'. Jean is particularly critical that the Indians had been paid 'in full' before the start, a custom he deplored. Be that as it may, Isabela's grand contingent of forty-one companions had shrunk to ten. The previous nine days have been terrible. The future, most abruptly, looked even bleaker.

Isabela and her group presumed that someone in her father's party had been carrying the disease. Its virulence had then incubated in a Canelos individual, or in several, before the tell-tale rash and fever informed everyone that the much-loathed viruela was striking once again. In their haste to flee the area its Canelos inhabitants had taken the canoes. They had also set fire to buildings in a desperate attempt to purify the air. Isabela and her party were therefore without good accommodation, without means of transport, without paddlers and even without much idea what they should do. To have longed so desperately for Canelos, and then to have all those high hopes dashed so speedily, must have been a most dismal experience. To spend that first night within the husk of a building, the stench of smoke all around them and none of the hospitality they had expected, was surely sufficient to bring them all to the brink of despair.

It did nothing of the sort for Isabela. Until that moment, cosseted at home, carried by palanquin from Baños, and assisted at every turn down the ravine, she had been a woman expecting the help which was her due. At Canelos, in that frightful situation, she started to show the steel in her temperament. This may have been forged, in part, by the loss of her own children to the disease. However much her family and friends had then rallied to lend support that misery had been a solitary experience. Such a wealth of unhappiness can turn individuals into pulp. It can also temper the material with which they are endowed, stiffen their resolve, and transform them into people of more solid substance than they had been previously.

At Canelos Isabela did not wither into a kind of nothingness. She was the undisputed leader of her party, and she therefore took the lead. Her father was waiting for her further downstream. The boat was waiting for her, and so was her husband at Cayenne. She had travelled across the dreadful cordillera, and was firmly on her way, with no wish to return to Riobamba. She refused to let herself be diverted by a mishap at the start. To yield at this first hurdle would be pathetic, and achieve nothing

117

whatsoever. As Jean phrased this moment in her life (a touch indulgently) 'the urge to join the boat, this ordered for her by two sovereigns, and the wish to see her husband again after twenty years absence, made her face all the obstacles'.

After a miserable night, she despatched the male members of her party to look for anything which might help. Not far from Canelos they encountered two Indians, both former residents of that community. These men gave news of the epidemic, and told how swiftly it had ravaged through the settlement. They were suspicious of the new arrivals, and fearful, but were cajoled into meeting Isabela. She encouraged them with money, paying them on the spot and in advance if they could find, or make, some form of transport to help her party on its way.

They did reveal the existence of a large canoe in need of repair, and offered to make it serviceable. This single craft was hardly what her father had in mind, and a crew of two frightened Indians was not what he had planned, but there were no more canoes and certainly no more Indians. With her party of eleven, and the two Indian paddlers, there was insufficient space for all the food and household goods they had carried through the ravine. Therefore some of this had to be abandoned, but the distance to Andoas was not great, twelve or so days of down-river travel, and the Bobonaza's urgent flow was encouraging, assuring everyone that the next mission station would soon be reached.

The Indians took control of the forty-foot canoe, laden with provisions and with thirteen souls on board.

Everyone was glad to put Canelos behind them, and their prospects looked a great deal brighter. The river enthusiastically hurried them along at a flow of five knots. All such river voyaging can be enchanting, and is particularly so for those recently switched from arduous progress on foot. The relative effortlessness is a joy. The jungle confusion on each bank is still dominant, but conveniently at a distance. Those spiky tangles, that mayhem, that huge and fallen tree, can all be observed so very casually. They are no longer obstacles to be overcome, and then succeeded by other hazards no less irksome. Indeed there is extra pleasure in seeing such hindrances from afar, and savouring their impotence.

Amazonian river travel is rich with virtues on its own account. The trees can look magnificent, with the tall giants so dominant and often buttressed for support. At every season some are in flower, with bright yellow or bright scarlets scattered amongst the green. The actual banks are often overhung with other colours, where ground-level plants can take advantage of a bright sun overhead. Here and there, keeping sentinel, are herons, motionless until they strike. Turtles keep them company, often on low-lying branches for many hours each day. Energetic otters abruptly raise their heads, sun-bitterns scramble up the banks, skimmers perform their graceful antics, and monkeys leap on high, with the howlers yelling raucously. Kingfishers forever hurtle across the river, descending almost to its level before swooping up to reach their favoured twigs. Beneath them, generally at the river's edge, are the snouts of caymans, sometimes big, usually small, ever ready for bonuses to come their way. Now and then, but most frequently at dawn and twilight, pairs or flocks of parrots and macaws fly overhead, squawking as if in protest to make their presence known, and travelling straight so very speedily.

Whether Isabela's party took note of the delights surrounding them, or were quite uncaring, they were probably most involved with the difficulties in their way. Meandering streams eat at banks alternately, perpetually carving a slightly different route. Riverside trees on eroded banks are steadily undermined until, one day, they fall. If previously magnificent, standing a hundred feet above the ground, they become a far less magnificent hazard reaching a hundred feet into the river's width. Water flows through their branches with undiminished haste, and water-borne travellers must make certain they do not follow suit. When suddenly confronted by such fallen trees all paddlers must coerce their craft to reach the river's other side. And they must always be alert for signs of trees beneath the surface. Their topmost branches may seem to be waving greetings, but are merrily indicating that a lot more tree is invisible beneath and very dangerous.

Rapids are another difficulty in the headwaters of the Amazon, able to break up the day quite disastrously. From water level, and a canoeist's height, these are not conspicuous, but distantly do give warnings of their existence which, once learned, are carefully remembered. The single blessing of lesser rapids is their shallowness. Crewmen can leap overboard, stand in the water, and manoeuvre their craft into a better position for going with the flow.

Isabela's journey, whether a matter of enjoyment or of concern, continued without any major problem for the first two days of their passage to Andoas. When darkness loomed each evening the Indians proposed a campsite. The air was warm and food was plentiful; morale was high. Of particular importance was the daily distance they had travelled. There was a growing sense of accomplishment during those first two days. The Andes were well behind them, and nothing but a length of river lay before them and the waiting galiot.

When everyone woke on the third morning of their river journey the Indians had departed. The mood of Isabela's party altered with similar haste. There was still food, and their single craft was where it had been moored, but the pilots had abandoned ship. Isabela's companions, now shrunk to ten again, were much less proficient for the task in hand. Future travel on the river would not be the elegant procedure which Don Pedro had organized; nor would it even imitate the departure from Canelos two days earlier. Far from being a luxurious experience, or a sensible compromise, the trip was becoming a survival enterprise, with a successful outcome no longer guaranteed.

Nevertheless Isabela's diminished gathering was still in good shape. Everyone was fit. Her two brothers, Joachim and the three Frenchmen would have to be in charge of navigation. Not one was expert, but all would have to do their best. The French were particularly apprehensive,

121

with the well-funded cruise they had anticipated now changed so dramatically. Instead of sitting in relaxed fashion while Indian paddlers did the work they would have to achieve much of it themselves. Therefore the doctor suggested turning back and at once came head to head with Isabela. She had not abandoned her home, her friends, and her birthplace only to return abjectly because some trouble had occurred. Moreover she had a husband to meet, and a father, and a galiot arranged on her behalf. She was therefore adamant. There would be no going back, even if such a return journey was actually feasible against the current. Forwards and downstream was the only way to go.

The Frenchman named Pierre offered to act as helmsman and, for the whole of that third day after leaving Canelos, all went well. Once more the forest passed them by on either bank, sometimes at five knots or so, and sometimes faster. Turtles still balanced on convenient branches. Caymans continued to stare unblinkingly from beneath the banks, and occasional capybaras leaped, either in major families or lesser groups, from the shore into the water, these colossal rodents being at home in either element. Swallows and martins sped by with their normal urgency, and a heron or two flapped east or west or elsewhere for better pickings in some other place. All was going satisfactorily, and better by far than they had dared to hope. Perhaps they possessed some expertise after all. They certainly went to sleep that night in a relaxed fashion, knowing that Andoas was now only some nine days distant.

On the following morning, their fourth since leaving the horror of Canelos, they saw a much smaller canoe moored next to a modest hut. Better still its Indian occupant, convalescing from some ailment, offered to join Isabela's party, and take the helm. Morale, forever a fickle accomplice, therefore rose again. Provisions were still plentiful. Everyone was in good health. Their canoe was in sound hands once again, and the forest once more passed by in casual fashion, with its attendant caymans and herons, its innumerable capybaras and, overhead, the raucous flights of parrots and macaws.

Mishaps tend not to give notice of their arrival. One of the French trio, relaxed in the canoe, lost his hat to a sudden breeze. The Indian, sitting and steering at the rear, saw it land in the water, and leaned to reach it. Unfortunately he leaned too far, and fell into the river. The man was not strong enough, as Jean recounts this incident, to climb back on board, and he therefore drowned. Presumably the canoe continued downstream, with or without an attempt at rescue. Either in these manoeuvrings or shortly afterwards the vessel filled with water. The survivors managed to bring it to the nearest bank and built a small shelter for themselves, a leaf-rooted *carbet* in Jean's description. Within its protection Isabela's bedraggled party chose to call it a day, and soon settled down to sleep. Don Pedro could never have believed his well-laid plans were going so awry.

From being reasonably placid, and half a mile wide in places, the Rio Bobonaza had become more violent. This may have been the cause of the canoe's upsetting in their inexpert hands. Moreover no one knew what might be in store further down the river. It could well become shallower, meaning a greater quantity of rapids and manoeuvring. It is easy to imagine that no one relished further journeying. Isabela's diminished party dried their clothes, ate a portion of the remaining food, and wondered what next to do. Every single one of them, as a most unwelcome possibility, could possibly succumb to whatever further mishap came their way.

A Greek tragedy ensnares its victims; they writhe but cannot escape. The Fates are in control and, whatever decision is taken by mere mortals, they remain in charge. Isabela and her party who had done nothing wrong since leaving Riobamba, were in such a predicament. Their options were not numerous, and none was attractive. Sitting on the river bank and hoping help might come by was one possibility. Travelling overland was another, but land travel was more difficult than the river. Replenishing their food supply was something else to do which would make the waiting more constructive. They could then build some better sort of home and create a kind of life, much as settlers do in any new environment. But there was one additional alternative, suggested by the Frenchman, Rivals. Why did he not take one of his fellow countrymen and paddle the canoe downriver to Andoas? The craft would be easier to navigate, and keep upright, with only two men and hardly any stores on board. Then, after collecting help from Andoas, the two of them would return, suitably equipped with more canoes and food.

Isabela Godin did not initially welcome this idea. Her younger brother, Eugenio, was also not in favour. Losing the canoe would leave the remaining members of the party extremely vulnerable. Isabela also did not relish the French suggestion that her voyage, and her party, should be in the hands of two individuals whose status on her expedition was least significant and least welcome. Unfortunately, as she reluctantly realized, all other options were even less appealing. She consented only on condition that Joachim should accompany the Frenchmen. At least her interests, and those of her family, would be uppermost in his mind. It was true that a large canoe with only three on board, and hardly any baggage, would not only ride higher in the water but be more manoeuvrable. With luck the canoe would make good time, and soon reach the downstream mission station at Andoas. If all went well they would be back, most probably, within fifteen days of their departure.

In Jean Godin's letter to La Condamine he rebukes his wife for being so trusting. The Frenchmen and Joachim took some food with them from the diminishing provisions, but also many of Isabela's valuables. These items had not been mentioned thus far in Jean's account, but Isabela had brought from Riobamba some of her more precious objects, such as gold plate and silverware. This burden would not have been a problem had everything occurred as it had been arranged, and she now chose to despatch the bulk of it with the departing canoe. Jean also wondered why, as additional security, she had not asked one of her brothers to accompany Joachim and the Frenchmen. But it appears they had been unwilling to entrust themselves to the river again, having seen what it could do. Therefore, as the French pair were willing and even eager, and Joachim was ordered on board, only these three were in the canoe when it was paddled downstream from the pitiful encampment.

With their departure the deserted encampment became increasingly bereft. What could they now do to help themselves? Two weeks are an eternity when there is nothing to do save glance downstream at the river bend and hope to see canoes being paddled urgently against the current. Isabela and her diminished party knew their waiting would have an end, most emphatically, if that help did not arrive.

Food gathering, already mentioned, is no easy matter anywhere in Amazonia. Brazil's famous nut most effectively symbolises the problem of finding forest food. When falling from the mature tree it is a cannon-ball, some four to five inches in diameter. Recalcitrant slaves were sometimes pegged beneath such trees as a form of punishment. To be hit on the head could well be fatal. To be missed, by inches or even feet, would most certainly be terrifying. Only one animal, the small and slender acouchi, possesses the teeth and cunning to sever through this nut's external casing, leaving the object then resembling a decapitated hard-boiled egg. Inside that shell, neatly packed without space to spare, are all the smaller nuts with which the world is more familiar. Even these have hard shells, although far less formidable than the solid casing which contained them. For humans, armed with machetes or convenient rocks, the opening of these cannon-balls is never simple. The knack can be acquired, given time, but emphasizes the problem of finding sustenance within Amazonia. The task is never easy.

It was not easy even for the Indian inhabitants until some had learned of agriculture, of growing manioc, of planting and cultivating nut-palms or other rewarding species near their settlements. The discovery of curare, made from lianas, permitted arrows and blow-pipe darts to be much more deadly. So too the stunning substances which bring fish to the water's surface, or woven fish-traps in chosen areas, or other devices discovered by one generation and passed on to the next. Isabela's group of Peruvians, so marooned on their piece of bank, were not forest individuals. They were town people, accustomed to acquiring food from markets, using money, bartering from time to time, and with little or no idea how to exist and prosper in the natural world.

During that first Sunday, still assuming they had left Canelos on the previous Monday, initially they could assuage their appetites after the canoe's departure. And so they could on the days which followed, although increasingly conscious that stocks were shrinking. With every day that passed, and yet more so when two weeks had been consumed, they were certainly aware that no form of help had come, and no one had appeared from that downstream river bend. The two weeks of waiting then stretched further, with no one bothering to keep the tally. The stores had initially been apportioned, as if fourteen days would be the length of waiting time. With the passing of that period, the group's disposition must have changed from impatience to misery, and then to deep despair. How many times must each of them, quite independently, have glanced downstream while longing for someone to be paddling their way?

Little was subsequently recorded about their life on that river bank. Some wood was gathered, with a fire always satisfactory for warming souls as well as bodies. Searches for food were surely undertaken, with tubers sought, and fond hopes arising that birds' eggs might be found, or fruit, or anything to quell a growing hunger and unease. Most certainly they did not venture far from the dwelling they had constructed, it is so easy to lose bearings among the trees. All awareness of direction is speedily disrupted – by some thicker than average entanglement, by major barriers, by anything in the way. There was probably no visible sun, and therefore no directional assistance from the sky, but even the ground could be unhelpful by undulating most unevenly. During previous centuries and millennia all nearby and meandering rivers have changed course time and time again. While doing so they have carved out new channels, built up new banks, and then moved elsewhere to leave a wavy landscape in their wake. Once each river has departed there is no longer such erosion, and the forest, after it has taken hold with its multitude of roots, tends to preserve the uneven shapes which it inherited. Therefore all walking uphill from a river's course can soon become downhill and then uphill once again. For any beginner, as with everyone of Isabela's party, the forest can become a mystery within a minute or two of entering its dark domain.

An English doctor, wishing to spend an Indian day within the trees of Amazonia, found a willing accomplice, watched him aim with a blow-pipe at some bird, saw it fall, and looked as this booty was cached within the crevice of a tree. The Englishman, panting to keep up with his strolling Indian partner, became increasingly exhausted as the day progressed. Suddenly, to his amazement, the same tree was once again in front of them. In his halting Portuguese this doctor asked a simple question, entirely valid at the time. 'How did you know where the tree was?' The Indian, previously curious about his companion and now utterly perplexed, replied straightforwardly: 'It was in the same place.' Strangers do find it easy to be lost within a forest, and it is likely that none of Isabela's companions wandered far from their makeshift home. If they did, and did become temporarily disorientated, they surely did not stray so far again.

There was also the problem of biting insects. Many Indian tribes have discovered effective repellents within the vegetation. Urucu from certain seeds is one example. But the party from Riobamba would have none of this vital knowledge. Much of the insect world is only active at certain times, such as dawn and dusk, when mosquitos mainly do their work. South America's rain forest, so well known for its multiplicity of species, can be venomous at almost any hour. Mosquitos certainly suck blood at both ends of the day, as do the far smaller sand-flies. Pium attack in daylight, preferring bright sunshine, and always leave great itching as reminders of their visits. There are also half-inch-long tabanids which make even cattle jump when injecting their biting apparatus and there are near-invisible blood-suckers whose previous presence is only indicated after tell-tale blotches appear on the skin. Ticks are a ubiquitous assortment, always ready to bite, with the largest of their kind most repulsive and the smallest most annoying. Every kind of bite is bad, but the subsequent itching, scratching and bacterial infection can be far more irritating and also damaging. Blisters can appear where only pimples used to be, and these can then suppurate most disgustingly. In short, forested Amazonia is a difficult place in which to maintain good health.

With Isabela's party her young nephew, Joaquín, was first to show signs of distress. His worsening condition was a major cause for Isabela to consider that something should be done other than waiting by the river's side for help that never came. After twenty-five days, and with food supplies much reduced, there was a corresponding increase in anxiety. Just what was going on down-river? Had the canoe even reached Andoas, or had its crew perished on the way? Perhaps the community of Andoas had proved to be as deserted as Canelos had been. Or had refused assistance. Or had no spare canoes, or Indians. Just what, if anything, was happening, and would a rescuing party soon come round that bend, or would one never do so, the river current too severe, the obstacles too numerous, the problems overwhelming? Joaquín might die if help was unavailable. For his sake, if for no other reason, something should be done.

Isabela therefore ordered the construction of a raft. It cannot have been very functional, since they had no tools to shape the logs and certainly no experience to help them bind the lianas. However, as on numerous occasions in other circumstances, there is undeniable relief in doing something rather than – which may be the wisest course – doing nothing whatsoever. Before long they had completed a raft to the best of their ability, and moved this to the water's edge. They placed on board most of their surviving stores, and the four women sat centrally nearest to these goods. Isabela held the sick child on her lap, and urged departure. The three men used poles to push this raft into the flow, and the next stage of their journey began.

Slender and well-made canoes are hard enough to steer in a speedy current, past rocks, past trees, and past all submerged obstacles if these are seen in time. A raft of any kind is relatively impossible to navigate, and becomes harder still when the river bottom is too deep for poles to be effective. As for its virtues, the raft can ride over sunken branches, if these are not too great, and may swivel around rocks when striking them. If stuck fast, and not too embedded on the rocks, good pole-work from appropriate vantage points can set the raft in motion once again. This can be an ungainly and testing form of travel, but at least provides movement of a jerky and haphazard sort. It therefore seemed to Isabela and her group as they progressed a great improvement on merely sitting still. In consequence some happy thoughts of arrival at Andoas surely surfaced in every one of them.

An underwater tree was then their undoing with frightening speed. It held them fast, and the strong current did its best to urge them onwards. These two ingredients, an immoveable tree and an urgent river, caused the raft to tip. The thing then broke apart, its poor construction proving quite inadequate to the test. Everyone was flung into the river, along with all their goods. Fortunately, this being the only luck to come their way that day, the bank was once again not far from their upsetting. They struggled towards it. Isabela was helped by her two brothers after she had twice vanished from their view, and eventually everyone, utterly drenched and gasping with relief, lay panting on the ground. The raft had taken them such a little distance that they were able to crawl back to their makeshift hut. This time they could not gather food or possessions but at least the eight of them had survived. They were all alive during that unhappy evening and when night arrived to cover up their wretchedness, but only seven of them were still living when the new dawn came.

Joaquín had died.

CHAPTER 9

The Sole Survivor

1769–70

Joaquín had died in his aunt's arms. For a long time she must have cradled him, hoping for some miracle to breathe life back into the silent form. Isabela certainly felt extra grief for ordering the construction of that raft. She had yielded to the temptation of doing something rather than sitting still. Her wish for action was understandable at the end of so many tedious days, but the boy had been poorly before that final embarkation. Without doubt his immersion in the water, and struggle to reach security, had helped to curtail his tenuous hold on life. To die within a few hours of that capsizing was proof, if proof were needed, that it had hastened his conclusion. Isabela knew all about watching children die, hers having so separately departed. At each of those times she had had the warmth of her home, her family, her closest friends. Now, despite her brothers and those three servants, she assuredly felt most wretchedly alone in the middle of her grief.

133

The fact of his leaving Riobamba was entirely her responsibility. This was her expedition. Due solely to her wish to meet her husband once again it had been organized. The sorry situation now surrounding them was at her behest, and she was powerless to improve it. What else could she have done at Canelos save appropriate the only craft they saw? Then, having met the underwater tree, and having foundered, what other choice was there on offer, save to despatch the canoe downriver with three on board to bring some urgent help? The construction of a raft had been misguided, but this further option had seemed wise, even if it had then become disastrous. What on earth was happening downstream? It was twenty-six days since the trio had departed. The canoe had surely met with something insuperable, causing its crew to die as a result. Therefore what had been the point of waiting for assistance with no one knowing of their plight? They had had to make a move themselves, but now could not build another raft, possessing neither energy nor will. All their food had gone, and they were as far from Andoas as they had been formerly, having done nothing but worsen their misery. What would happen now at their miserable little camp in the midst of a hostile world? And what would become of them?

Joaquín had died, and was not even buried. No one had the strength to make a hole for him. As for tossing his lifeless body into the river that was not an option. Instead he lay as one horrible reminder of a pitiful predicament. The sight prompted Isabela to suggest they attempt to make progress by walking along the river bank. Jean Godin reports his astonishment at this choice in his later letter to La Condamine. 'What an undertaking! You know, Sir, that the banks of these rivers are lined with thickets, creepers, bushes, where one can only obtain light by cutting with a sickle and losing so much time.'

Jean's presentiments were correct, but he did not appreciate the party's desperation. In any case, river-bank travel was soon abandoned as impossible and they returned to their original location with its makeshift hut. No longer did anyone now bother to look at the down-stream bend for a rescuing canoe; that hope had long since gone. Instead they soon set off on foot once more. Realising that any attempt to follow the river's meandering course only added distance to their progress, this time they entered the forest itself, but after a short time, as Jean writes most casually, 'they were lost'. Most assuredly they were. They were certainly lost within an hour, or even within a shorter time. Their feet 'were stung by thorns and brambles'. They found 'some seeds and wild fruit' but became increasingly hungry. And thirsty too. And exhausted. And when that short time had passed, 'tired by so much walking in a harsh thick wood [they] gave up, sat down, and could not rise again'. They had come to the end of their rope.

Lying there, sometimes sleeping, and occasionally moving, they each faced their end. For the maid Heloise a solution came to her befuddled mind. She wandered from the encampment and was never seen again. Her disappearance was scarcely noticed. As for Rosa, the oldest of the three servants, she soon died quietly in her sleep. Elvia was still alive, half-aware of these tragedies but only distantly, as were Isabela, her brothers and the remaining Frenchman. The end of their lives was advancing towards them, most straightforwardly, and without a hint of opposition. It was merely marking time.

Joachim, the faithful servant of his much-admired patroness, had experienced awesome difficulty in his second crucial mission on her behalf. He had not died, as Isabela had feared; nor had the canoe come to grief. Instead there had merely been intransigence. On reaching Andoas, the Frenchmen had made it plain they had no intention of returning upstream on a rescue mission, and it took time for Joachim on his own to persuade the fathers at the mission that help should be provided for half a dozen people stranded on the Bobonaza river bank, nearly 200 miles upstream.

Joachim did eventually set off in a single canoe, equipped with Indian paddlers and a quantity of food. Those familiar with the area, such as the Andoas missionaries, considered that at least eight days would be necessary before the rescue party could hope to reach its objective, but at least, and at last, help was on its way. Joachim had no idea what he would find when he eventually arrived, but he had done his best. Almost a month had passed since he had seen his lady Isabela, and he surely urged his Indian paddlers to greater haste as they struggled against the flow.

When the twelve-year-old nephew Joaquín died, and the others did not, or could not, bury him, his corpse had been terrible affirmation of each survivor's plight. Death was the single certainty. In time, in very little time, its revulsion would embrace them all. By now there were only five still living at that resting place within the forest – the two brothers, the surviving maid-servant, the final Frenchman, and Isabela Godin. One by one the sweet caress of nothingness would take them in its care. For those that lasted longest the sight of bodies so near at hand, and then the stench so quickly all-pervading, did not so much prepare them for certain ends as encourage them to succumb, without thought, without misery, and without much comprehension. Isabela might have wondered how a proud gathering of forty-two could have descended so speedily, and so abjectly, into a lonely group of five without any spirit left to live. She herself was sinking equally. Her older brother Antoine was absent-mindedly telling his beads when he expired. The Frenchman then died and so did Elvia. They had been lying, moribund, inert, until – without any outward change – they were simply lying there. Isabela and her younger brother Eugenio knew their time would come. Small creatures which had been feasting on the living continued to prey on the dead as decay proceeded with tropical swiftness.

Isabela, who had composed herself, as had the others, for whatever came to pass, suddenly awoke from her abstraction. She had spent some two days in a distant reveric, aware of nothing, before the stench assaulted her. It was loathsome and most foul. Making everything yet more repellent was the fact that it came from those she loved. She sat up, appalled by everything so near at hand. Somehow she alone had come back to life, affronted by the smell and sight. She knew she had to leave.

With a knife she cut the shoes from a dead brother, and fashioned these into sturdier sandals for herself. She also found a machete, and picked a stick for support. From being inert and helpless she became transformed into an active being, far from a replica of her former self but quite dissimilar from the expiring object she had been when lying on the ground. She had no idea where to go, or what to do. Her single purpose was to exist somewhere else, away from the horrendous smell, away from the spectacle which was creating it. The love she had felt for the former beings had become a loathing; she therefore had to go.

As she stumbled from the scene, deranged and distraught, she even imagined that someone was calling her name. In amongst the bird calls and other animal shrieks, and in amongst her staggering and slithering over rotting twigs, she heard this insane cry. Or she thought she did. Nothing was truly real in that predicament, not the forest all around her, not even her wretched body taking her somewhere else. Nightmares have no sense to them, even when in daytime they are real. The body's senses feed in information, but are confused with disbelief. What they are detecting cannot actually be happening, not ever, and certainly not then. Yet the cry persisted as she plunged deeper and deeper into that dark embrace of trees. 'Isabela, Isabela,' came the cry until it was quietly ended. Then nothing but the forest, with all its sounds and silences, was surrounding her. Beforehand she had been lonely. Now she was entirely on her own, most absolutely on her own.

It may well have been that Isabela Godin did hear Joachim's voice calling her name, with so many dates in this story so imprecisely known. In Jean Godin's letter to La Condamine he is clearly uncertain, stating that Isabela's disappearance within the forest occurred 'around the 25th to the 30th of December 1769'. The servant Joachim had no accurate idea how many days or weeks he had spent travelling downstream with the French pair, speaking with the Andoas missionaries, persuading them to send relief, and then proceeding upstream to the place where he had last seen his mistress. It is also not known, most understandably, quite how long Isabela and her group had spent in their makeshift camp before choosing to create a raft. As for the number of days that passed after the terrible capsizing, after young Joaquín had died, and when others were dying around her, Isabela had even less idea of passing time. And she assuredly had no understanding how long she had lain there, seemingly moribund, before the awful quantity of death had pricked her into consciousness. Therefore, after adding all those unknown lengths of time together, it could well have been that Joachim's re-arrival at the camp and Isabela's vanishing in the forest were more or less simultaneous. Fate can play such tricks, timing everything so neatly and so irritatingly that possible reunions very nearly occur but do nothing of the sort.

For days and days, following his departure from Andoas, Joachim must have urged his paddling Indians to greater haste. Every time they halted, to rest, to fish for food, or to roast their catch over open fires, he must have fretted at the enforced delay. Would he recognize the camp? He might have wondered if the canoe, paddled so urgently upstream, had overshot the mark. Only he knew how the makeshift dwelling on the bank had been constructed, and how its slippery bank had differed from all others, but the Indians with him would surely be adept in recognising where humans had spent time. The paddling therefore continued, with Joachim's anxiety steadily rising rather than diminishing, until suddenly, with all of them seeing the place at once, they came across the camp. It did not look quite as Joachim remembered. The group had lived there for almost a month after his departure. But it was certainly what he and the canoeists had been seeking during all their upstream days.

Joachim would have been first out of the canoe, slipping on the mud, holding on to roots, scrambling up the bank, and then being horror-struck at the sight of a single and decaying corpse. The ten-year-old boy, never buried, must have been in a terrible condition. Whether Joachim recognized those remains is not known, but he surely saw that only one body was involved, and must have wondered about the remainder. He may have shouted Isabela's name or he may have been utterly silenced both by the spectacle and the realisation that, for one person at least, his arrival with assistance had come too late.

Meanwhile the Indians were exploring the path which Isabela and her unhappy group had made when abandoning the dead boy and seeking solace in the forest. Very quickly they came upon the spot where so much death had taken place. Joachim's horror was now total. They were all dead. Having been entrusted to bring aid he had failed most comprehensively. By now there could have been no question of him calling any name. All he could see was death, and he had been responsible. The group he had left behind had undoubtedly died from a lack of sustenance, and he had let them down. To witness the corpses was bad enough. To feel guilty about their endings certainly made the sight infinitely worse.

What Joachim did not do was count the carcasses lying on the ground. Perhaps large animals had been at the bodies, scattering limbs and clothing, making such a calculation difficult. He certainly failed to notice that one of the three maid-servants was absent, and he did not observe that Isabela was also elsewhere. Neither did the Indians point to any marks which she might have made when departing from that place. No one can make passage inconspicuously through the tangled growth by a river bank, this being so thick, but the inside of a forest is much easier to penetrate. A lack of light means a lack of growth, save for trees sufficiently tall to reach it. To walk between the trees, and over the leaves that carpet such an area, is probably to leave no signs behind. Or at least no signs for those not expecting them. Perhaps Joachim and the others deliberately did not search for further information, with their eyes hating to take any additional note of the scene in front of them.

As for her black servant the sight of Doña Isabela's corpse, had she been there and then identified, would have been the most unsettling and most gruesome of them all. That lady, after rescuing him from bondage, had given him a better life. All he had done, as miserable reward, was to arrive too late. He had been at fault, and yet he was still alive. The stench, and sight, and horror, was entirely due to him. Consequently he did not, and could not, linger there, the place so rich with blame. Without any more ado, having collected some abandoned possessions still lying in the hut, they all hurried back to the canoe and paddled off downstream.

On returning to Andoas Joachim would have to inform the missionaries. They would then send the news down-river to Don Pedro at Lagunas. Isabela's father would be utterly bereft, not only to have lost his precious daughter, but two sons and a grandson as well. All had departed in this terrible tragedy. Like Joachim he too would be engulfed in remorse. Why had he not returned to accompany his daughter's party through the Andes, and then down-river? How had his plans, which he had thought sufficient, gone so wretchedly wrong? He had heard nothing of the smallpox, and had had no suspicion of any problem until the information from Andoas which told him, so brutally and so suddenly, of so much death.

As for the patient boatmen of the galiot they would learn that everything had been in vain, their visit to Cayenne, their journey upstream, and then their four-year wait.

This dreadful information would then have to proceed further down-river, with such news travelling so very speedily, first to Iquitos, then Pará, and finally around to Cayenne in French Guiana. Jean Godin's long wait, and his ignorance about almost everything, would finally be ended. In one horrific package he would learn of the death of his wife, of all their children, of his brothers-in-law, of a nephew, and of other members of his Peruvian house-hold. He would also be informed of the galiot's per-severance on his behalf, and he too would have been assaulted by remorse along with all his grief. What would have happened if he had believed Rebello, and had travelled upstream with that galiot to the Andes? Would any of the tragedy have occurred had he, the veteran of South American travel, as he had labelled himself, been able to assist that up-river enterprise instead of frittering his time away so uselessly in France's colony? His twenty years of waiting had been quite pointless, and fatuous, and a great waste of life. There was nothing more to do, save return to France, without a wife, without children, and deeply burdened with his guilt.

Isabela's abrupt departure from the place of death is as comprehensible as Joachim's near-immediate vanishing.

The forest around her was hardly welcoming, but anything and anywhere was better than that charnel house. The reek was one revulsion, but the sights were equally horrendous, the buzz of flies, the grey-green colouring of skin, and the ungainly postures, perhaps nudged this way and that by various creatures seeking flesh. She must have hurried from the scene as fast as she was able. She must also have had no plan, save to put distance between herself and all that dreadfulness.

At once, therefore, she would have lost her bearings. Ordinary individuals, unassailed by any form of trauma, quickly fail to know in which direction they are heading. There are no clues, at least none for those whose forest experience is almost nil. Even if the sun is shining the leaf canopy makes its position a matter of guesswork rather than clarity. There is also a sombre gloom within the forest, with less than one-hundredth of the light at higher levels reaching the ground below. Isabela, quite unacquainted with that arboreal world, would very quickly not have known where to go, and in which direction, to leave the dreadfulness still further in her wake.

There is nothing quite like a stumble to increase disorientation. There is also nothing quite like a rain forest for making travellers miss a footing. Fallen branches, each glistening with moisture, can offer no resistance whatsoever to a foot or feet, particularly when those extremities are encased in shoes. Naked feet are more capable, but only if experienced in their nakedness. Isabela's feet, with sandals on their soles, needed the covering, and would have paid the price again and again by slithering and sliding so very frequently. Each time, however speedily she then clambered up again, she would have been less certain in which direction she should go. Or had been going before the fall.

To lie down in the forest is to yield, wholesale, to insect life. This will either take advantage – by biting, sucking, probing – or casually accept a chance to inspect, up nostrils, within ears, by eye-balls, wherever it chooses. The ticks are also opportunist, whether sizeable or small. The smallest, in their hundreds, welcome sweaty crevices, with human navels a favoured destination. Whether Isabela greatly cared about such pin-pricks to her welfare is not known, but she was certainly assaulted by much of the multi-legged world she now inhabited.

What she should have done, had she possessed her former sanity, was to find a stream, watch its water-flow, follow that downhill path, encounter bigger streams, and then eventually meet some river. No one had homes in that area unless it was well equipped with water. Only by travelling downstream could she hope to find a settlement, and only in such communities could she hope to find some food. Most certainly she was not acquiring it within the forest, not knowing how to take honey from the bees, how to discover nuts, how to eat from little palms, and how to find the eggs of birds. She was a stranger in that place, too forlorn and ignorant to make a living from it.

In his later letter to la Condamine Jean Godin gives certain details of his wife's forest nightmare. Initially he writes that 'Providence wishing to conserve her' was the reason she left her dead companions. At that time she was 'in a daze, distraught, and almost overwhelmed'. She was 'half-naked', dressed only in 'two mantillas and a tattered blouse [which] hardly covered her'. How could it be, asks this letter-writer, 'that a woman delicately brought up' might hope to survive in such a place? She would certainly not be feeding adequately, and her exhaustion would increase each day. Worst of all she had no aim. The only people in the area would be Indians, and not the tamed variety within the mission stations. What might they do to her in their savagery? Back in Riobamba there had been common talk of Indian atrocity, of heads shrunk, of living burial. She could not even fight if captured, being sapped of strength and with no weapon of defence. She would be the easiest of victims, ripe for anything they chose to do. They were to be dreaded, even more than the perils around about her.

Therefore she walked, and staggered, and stumbled on and on. What else was there for her to do, save lie down and hope for an early end? The one assistant in her peril was her faith. She did believe in a protector, knowing she had already been saved from death. She had to keep going, and earn the extra life she had been granted. There was no question of an abdication, not while she could stand, and move, and give her possible deliverance some form of opportunity, however this might occur.

Making everything more daunting was the eternal sameness of the forest landscape. There is no sense of progress, either up or down, as on mountainsides. Instead there is a perpetual undulation, more like the surging of the sea. Oceans never run short of waves, and the forest is equally unlimited, being the same in each direction, with huge trees on occasion and with lesser forms filling all the gaps. Where there might be sky, after a giant has tumbled to the ground, there is always a profusion of speedy growers taking up the space. The obstacles to be encountered are then even thicker. Therefore Isabela, without knowing what she was doing, would have avoided them. The path of least resistance is always chosen, whether at normal times or when deranged by misery. She cannot have known what was happening, being – in one historian's words – 'a woman of gentle soul, alone and lost in the most dreaded jungle in the world'.

For some nine days she was alone, as Jean later calculated, and for all that time she was entirely lost. She did apparently find some berries, and some green eggs – which Jean deduced 'were those of a kind of partridge'. These gave her little help as, 'hardly had she swallowed them than her oesophagus contracted from the lack of food'. In any case the nourishment which came her way was, in Jean's telling phrase, only 'sufficient to feed a skeleton'. It was high time, he asserted, if there was justice in the world, that the help so plainly due to her for all her perseverance actually arrived.

There was no purpose in her wandering, no longed for destination, and every day she was growing weaker.

Her scanty clothing had now left her, and her skin had become a patchwork of bites and scratches, of open sores and stiffened blood. What kept her going was the strong belief that deliverance would – somehow – come her way. She had lain down with the others, and they had died but she had not. She would keep going until neither spirit nor body could drive her any further. Until then she would pray for salvation from the miserable agony. Somehow assistance would come her way, provided she persevered.

One day she heard a voice, and then saw two men launching a canoe. This had been pulled up on the land, as is the custom for keeping a boat secure, and they were returning it to the water. They were forest Indians, and she immediately shrank in fright. They had apparently not seen her, and she stayed quite motionless. Indians were the enemy, and she was a woman alone. Formerly everything had been awful. Now there was only fear.

She stood, they moved, and a brand new thought then cavorted through her head. Why not end it all? In her stumbling passage through the trees she had been someone not yet dead, and the Indians were very much alive. What had she got to lose? She could not run, and could scarcely walk. They were the first people she had seen in all her wandering. A longing for company possibly inspired her more than a plea for help. It then appeared as if they might move away, and this emboldened her. She made a noise and began to move, causing both the Indians to glance her way. They stared most terribly, and then they were coming in her direction, the two of them quite silently, and no longer talking to themselves. This would be the end.

CHAPTER 10

Stranger Than Fiction

1770

Jean Godin permitted himself a short, if somewhat breathless, diversion in his lengthy letter addressed to Charles-Marie de la Condamine.

> If you read in a novel that a delicate woman, used to enjoying all the nice things of life, has fallen into a river, has been rescued when half-drowned, has then disappeared into a pathless wood before becoming lost after several weeks of walking while suffering from hunger, thirst and exhaustion, and has survived even the awful sight of the deaths of her two young brothers, much stronger than herself, of a nephew hardly out of childhood, and of the young valet of the doctor who has gone ahead; if you read that, after remaining alone for two nights and two days among those corpses, in districts where tigers and many dangerous serpents abound, she never meets one of them, and gets up to start

walking again with tattered clothes, roaming in a trackless wood up to the eighth day when she finds herself on the banks of a river, you would then accuse the novelist of not being true to life.

He does have a point. The tale was a tall one, particularly in the eighteenth century when women only rarely wandered from a clearly defined existence. Certainly none did so in Amazonia when middle-aged, and to survive younger and apparently fitter companions. Jean found the whole story astonishing, just as those two Indians with their canoe by that river bank must have been astounded at the sight of Isabela. They too may have been frightened, and certainly perplexed. The woman in front of them, plainly distraught, scarcely clothed, absolutely unkempt and covered in bites, was like no one they had ever seen. If they recognized her as European rather than Indian she was the first of her kind they had witnessed in such a state. They had possibly never seen any Indian woman so bedraggled, so haggard, and so alone. As for the Europeans they had encountered, whether male or female, young or old, they had never found them wandering through the forest, miserable, wretched, and undoubtedly in need of help. When they approached her she stayed rooted, not daring to move, and hardly able to do so.

Isabela had not initially noticed there were two women with the men, and certainly could never have foreseen the care these four then lavished on her. 'They covered my wife with affection,' wrote Jean. Her ability to speak

Quecha, the local tongue, undoubtedly helped, and she told them of her wish to reach Andoas. This proved to be no problem. The Indians, former residents of Canelos, had fled from that place when smallpox arrived. It was their intent, after spending time within the forest, to proceed on their own to Andoas. Isabela knew, with all this talk, and care, and warmth, that her faith in providence had been completely justified. She had not known how aid would come her way; she had only known it would do so. And then, with those four sympathetic Indians on their way to Andoas, it had arrived in splendid form.

The arrival at Andoas would be nothing like so wonderful. Its Jesuits had been replaced by a secular priest and the new man's attitude may have been one reason why Joachim had taken such time in arranging rescuers. Isabela wished to thank her Indian deliverers, but had nothing to offer save for two gold chains around her neck. According to Jean (often precise and clear about valuable items) these objects weighed four ounces. The priest resented her generosity, and substituted three lengths of the coarse cotton cloth known locally as tucuyo. This reward was markedly inferior in value, causing Isabela to be furious. Instead of resting and recuperating at the mission she immediately ordered a canoe and paddlers to take her down-river. The lack of humanity so blatantly displayed toward her rescuers was such an affront that departure was the only course. After receiving a cotton petticoat, fashioned for her by an Indian woman, she abandoned

Andoas on the very day of her arrival. For more than a month she had treasured the thought of reaching that community. Within minutes of arrival she had changed her mind entirely. The woman of gentle birth had an iron resolve when need be.

Meanwhile other events were taking place that were equally distasteful. Two individuals who might be presumed to have dropped out of the story emerged again, namely Tristan d'Oreasaval and 'the soi-disant médecin', Dr Rivals. Each had been proved unsatisfactory, and each continued to be so, not changing their spots in the slightest. The objects which Joachim had found in the abandoned riverside hut before his sad return to Andoas were not insignificant. Joachim had collected everything he found, and took it downstream with him after leaving Andoas. At a further mission station he met the alleged doctor and, following persuasion, handed over the objects he had gathered. Later on, when Rivals learned of Isabela's miraculous survival, and had appreciated that a journey by galiot might again be possible, he met his former patroness once more and handed over her possessions. Unfortunately, as Jean realized when piecing the story together, numerous items were missing. The doctor proffered 'four silver plates, one drinking pot, a velvet skirt, a 'Persienne' [skirt], a taffeta one, some linen and other clothes'. Everything else had allegedly suffered, this final statement making Jean incensed. 'The doctor . . . was forgetting that gold bracelets, gold snuff boxes, gold reliquaries, and emerald ear-rings never rot.' The Frenchman was guilty of theft, and the case against him could be proved by Joachim.

Unfortunately this servant had been despatched back to Quito by none other than the French doctor and the wretched Tristan d'Oreasaval. Those two chose to override Don Pedro's wishes to speak with Joachim and hear a full account of the dreadful happenings between deserted Canelos and inhospitable Andoas. Don Pedro had even 'commanded' d'Oreasaval to bring the former slave downstream. By then poor Joachim was returning across the Andes, having been instructed to depart. When Rivals was questioned about Joachim's dismissal, and asked why he had taken such a liberty, he told of his fear that 'the Negro might murder him'.

It is easy to understand why Joachim might have wished to end the doctor's life, but the explanation did not satisfy Jean. A servant, 'whose zeal and fidelity had been exemplary, should have been clapped in irons, and brought downstream', had the suspicions possessed any validity. There would have been no difficulty in imprisoning Joachim, had this been thought advisable, as the Frenchman was then staying with the governor of Omagua. 'You cannot imagine the excuses I have been trying to make for Monsieur R . . . in order to exonerate him' for having despatched such a valuable eyewitness. As it was the 'loyal and necessary servant [had] become lost', both to his mistress and to Jean – and to this story.

In many ways Joachim had been the hero of the Godin drama. He had been sent over the mountains to find the boat. He had failed once, and had succeeded on the second attempt. After a two-year stint he had returned to Isabela with the good news. He had undoubtedly been helpful on her own mountain journey, and had then been entrusted to bring back aid from Andoas for the beleaguered group on the river bank. Without his dogged devotion there would never have been a rescue party, and he could not be blamed for its tardiness. After finding the corpses he had then gathered the valuables, had handed them over as requested and, as reward for all his pains, had been banished back to Quito. No wonder that Jean Godin felt enraged, however belatedly. And no wonder he was miserable at losing touch with such a man.

Joachim had departed before Isabela Godin arrived at Lagunas. She then found herself in the care of a Dr Romero, the new Superior of the missions. He was lavish in his support, and had sent assistance up-river after her withdrawal from Andoas. He had also sent word down-river to the governor of Omagua about her survival, and the 'state of languor' in which she had arrived. The encounter between Isabela and Dr Rivals was extremely icy. 'If you had brought me back my Negro,' she declared, 'I would have known what he had done with the effects found in the shelter . . . Come on, Sir, it is not possible for me to forget that you are the originator of my misfortunes and my losses. I no longer wish to have you in my company.'

Her wrath and displeasure are understandable, but Dr Romero interceded on the doctor's behalf. This missionary, to whom Isabela 'could refuse nothing', said that if she abandoned the Frenchman 'he would return triumphant at her repulsion'. If Joachim was this tale's worthiest individual the soi-disant doctor was most certainly its villain, but Dr Romero's words found their mark. Isabela reluctantly agreed that the Frenchman could accompany her (an acceptance which presumably included the second Frenchman whose existence is no longer mentioned in Jean's narrative). The iciness towards both of them surely continued, however generous her act.

Six weeks passed before Isabela Godin felt sufficiently recovered to think about continuing her journey. One of her thumbs had been a particular problem. It had been impaled by thorns during her jungle wanderings, and an abscess had resulted. Even the tendons and bone in that area were affected, and there was initial talk of amputation. Fortunately, 'thanks to treatment and ointments', this proved unnecessary, and she experienced greatest pain during the operation to extract the offending material.

Isabela's father, already described as shadowy, is yet more so during this convalescent period. There is no description of his activities at this time. Neither is there information how he heard the news of his daughter's survival, nor where and when he met her once again. Don Pedro had, as it were, gained a daughter, but had also received terrible affirmation of so much death, of his two sons, of one grandson, and of three members of his household. He too was surely miserable that Joachim had been returned to Quito.

When Isabela had sufficiently revived Romero sent word to all concerned that she was out of danger. He also wrote to the local governor that it might be better for 'Madame Godin' to be returned to Riobamba. He praised her for her courage and devotion but, if she was to proceed further, she was only at the beginning of a long and tiresome voyage. Isabela had already travelled 'some 400 leagues' and still had 'four or five times as much' to reach Cayenne. She had escaped death narrowly and was about to be exposed to a whole new set of risks. In fact he, Dr Romero, would be happy to take her back 'in all security' to her residence in Riobamba.

Isabela was astonished by this proposition, and rejected it at once. 'God had preserved her from all the perils to which the others had succumbed', as Jean phrased it, and she had 'no other wish' than to rejoin her husband. She had set out with that intent, and had no desire to thwart the designs of providence. Nor had she any intent 'to render useless' the assistance she had received 'from the two dear Indians and their wives'. Similarly all the help she had already received from the unstinting Dr Romero, could not be set aside. She owed her life to these people, and only God knew how they should be rewarded. 'My wife has always been dear to me,' wrote Jean, but 'respect and tenderness' were now added. In many ways he hardly knew the person he had married, having spent six years with her in Riobamba and another twenty in quite a different land. When writing to La Condamine he was making his affections public. He could hardly say he was waiting for someone to whom he felt indifferent. The warmer his feelings, particularly those expressed out loud, the more his lengthy wait was justified.

So Dr Romero arranged for Tristan d'Oreasaval to conduct Isabela down-river to the Portuguese boat. But needless to say, knowing of Tristan's wayward behaviour with letters and money, he did not arrive to collect Isabela as had been requested. Dr Romero grew increasingly impatient, eventually despatching Isabela down-river by dug-out canoe to the 'bâtiment' of the King of Portugal, the nearest official building in Brazilian territory. If a dug-out sounds uncomfortable for days of continuous travel one should remember the luxurious vessel chartered by La Condamine and Maldonado. That had a rear roofed section, separated from the paddlers, and was most commodious. Presumably the lady Isabela was similarly transported and equipped.

From being so isolated in the forest she was now besieged by assistance. The down-river governor of Omaguas, on hearing that Isabela was travelling in his direction, sent a boat with 'a few refreshments' to meet her. This portion of the story, in Jean's account, becomes confused, with so many parties eager to render help, and with Isabela, her father, the French pair and even Tristan d'Oreasaval initially at different locations, that who met whom, and when and where, is difficult to disentangle. Perhaps it does not matter greatly as they all met in the end.

With great quantities of official assistance, and so much striving on her behalf, it might seem as if the King of

Portugal was himself arriving. The truth is that Isabela's story, the loss of her family, her salvation from the forest, and her determination to meet her husband touched everyone who heard the tale. It was courageous and inspiring, as well as providential. If ever a person needed assistance which had been so plainly earned, that was Isabela. The fact of it being a woman's story made it all the more remarkable. She had survived the forest, and young men with her had not. She was determined to carry on, despite past horrors and the distance still to be achieved. She was quite extraordinary, and therefore deserved every form of aid that could come her way.

This adventure involved so many facets in its accomplishment. Religion and faith were there most plentifully. So too Amazonia, with all its natural horrors. Politics were also relevant, with Spain, Portugal and France each involved. There were Indians, either to be feared or praised. There was death in abundance and astonishing survival. A total of forty-two individuals had set forth from Riobamba, and almost all of them had either vanished within the forest or had perished miserably. The two Frenchmen and Joachim were still living, but only because they had escaped the scene of tragedy. In a sense Doña Isabela was the sole survivor.

Even had her journey from the west of South America been plain sailing it would have been remarkable. Citizens of Peru did not frequently travel across the eastern Andes. Women 'of gentle birth' did so even less, and much less rarely if they had exceeded forty years. No one knew of any expedition in which such a miraculous survival had occurred. And no one would expect a frail woman to be the only individual to prevail of a group abandoned on a river bank. Of the forty-two people who had started from Riobamba no one knew the number still living a few months later. Its Indian contingent may well have been assaulted by smallpox. The former slave had been returned to Quito, and no one much cared for the two Frenchmen, their ignominious behaviour well reported.

That was the information which circulated around the mission stations, the colonising outposts, the isolated settlements east of the Andes, and that was the story which would travel downriver in advance of the single person who had emerged from a terrible tragedy. The facts surely improved with the telling, and then doubly so when it was realized that the entire endeavour, her entire endeavour, was in order to be reunited with her husband after a lapse of twenty years. What fidelity! What a providential happening! Above all, what a woman!

CHAPTER 11

A Joyful Reunion
1770–3

Isabela's downstream journey was to be more of a triumphal procession than the final leg of a transcontinental exploit. It was also to be a total contradiction of the earlier experience, when death and misery had been so abundant. On board would be not only Captain de Rebello and his patient oarsmen, but also the French doctor, the inexcusable Tristan d'Oreasaval and Isabela's father. Don Pedro, having lost two sons and one grandson, seems to have had no immediate desire to return home. As for the undeserving renegades, Tristan and the doctor, for whom space was also found, Isabela's compassion and willingness to forgive were plainly of the highest order. They had done her no good whatsoever, and she was providing them with 3,000 miles of effortless transport down the world's mightiest river.

From her embarkation onwards, according to the final paragraphs of Jean Godin's lengthy letter, his wife lacked nothing. The foods placed before her and her overall comfort 'were probably unequalled in such navigation'. It therefore sounds as if she did rather better than he did on his voyage. There were 'wines and liqueurs in abundance . . . for which she had no need', as well as ample provision of game and fish. Two boats went ahead of the galiot to collect 'desirables' which, one hopes, were also enjoyed by the long-suffering crew. The governor of Pará had sent orders upriver that full assistance should be given, and more and more '*rafraîchissements*' arrived from every quarter. If the first section of Isabela's travels had been hellish, the second, and longer, portion was a form of paradise unimaginable during those earlier days. The story of her survival caused admiration and delight. In consequence her journey down-river became a pageant more fitted for a queen.

Her change in circumstance was one of astonishment. So too was the venture as a whole. For a great quantity of time Jean Godin had been a forlorn individual in Guiana, much resented by the colony's governor, seemingly forgotten by the world, and leading an unhappy existence with little idea what best to do. Without much wisdom he had entrusted incriminating letters to the mayhem of Atlantic travel, and did not take advantage when a rowing boat arrived on his behalf. Then, in an eye's blink, after such a lengthy wait and such indifference, his wife was coming down the Amazon as if she were a royal personage, instead of being no more than the partner of a former chain-bearer attached to a half-forgotten foreign expedition.

A Joyful Reunion

Monsier de Martel, Knight of the Order of Christ, and major of the Pará garrison, had been ordered by Pará's governor to proceed to Gurupá to take over as the boat's commander from Captain de Rebello – who was, no doubt, amazed and most grateful to be ordered home. Gurupá lies on the northern branch of the Amazon's 200-mile wide delta, and is therefore a better staging post for journeys to Guiana than Pará on the southern side. De Martel's orders were to take Isabela directly to Oyapock, Jean Godin's home and the spot where he had abandoned ship some five years earlier.

Navigating a galiot on the edge of an ocean was much trickier than river travel. Shortly after leaving the delta's relative tranquillity, and on encountering an area famous for its violent currents, De Martel lost one of his two anchors. He considered it unwise to proceed further and chose to send a small launch (a 'chaloupe') to request assistance from Oyapock. Thus it was that Jean Godin heard of his wife's proximity. He had already learned of her disappearance and her presumed death, and subsequently of her astonishing survival, but the launch's arrival was immediate confirmation that all was indeed happening as he had been informed. His precious wife was on the other side of a place called Mayacaré, on the coast between Oyapock and the mouth of the Amazon.

Knowing of his previous caution concerning foreign vessels, and of his unwillingness to go on board, it is almost surprising to read in his letter to La Condamine that he wished to hasten the reunion by travelling to the stranded galiot. He decided to sail in his own 'galiote' for the encounter, and arrived in her presence 'on the fourth day' after leaving Oyapock. In his description of that occasion he permits himself a curious exuberance.

> Thus it was that after twenty years of absence, of alarms, of crossings, and mutual misfortunes, that I joined a darling wife I had never thought of seeing again. I forgot in our embraces the fruits of our marriage, and was even joyful that their early deaths had saved them from the fate which befell their uncles in the forest of Canelos. If they too had perished then in similar style their mother would never have survived that spectacle.

Jean Godin was almost more delighted by the distinguished officer in charge of the galiot, a man as proficient in his general knowledge as in his 'exterior advantages'. Monsieur de Martel was of French descent from the 'illustrious' family whose name he bore. Fluent in 'almost every European language' he was equally at home in Latin and, in Jean's opinion, could have shone on a bigger stage than that of Pará. At all events this individual, plainly brilliant and charming, brought Jean and Isabela to Oyapock, arriving there on 22 July 1770. At once a message was sent off *'par un éxprès'* to Monsieur de Fiedmond, Cayenne's governor, informing him that the reunion of Monsieur and Madame Godin des Odonais had finally been achieved.

This was the same governor with whom Jean Godin had crossed so many swords – by correspondence – in earlier years. Now he lavished assistance in their direction, presumably relieved that the whole saga was about to be concluded. As with everyone else in authority who had heard the Isabela story, he despatched a vessel to the galiot, filled with more '*rafraîchissements*'. The galiot itself also needed aid, such as a new hull and new sails to travel along the coast against the currents. This major refurbishment, understandably necessary after all those years at anchor up the Amazon, seems to have been achieved with commendable speed, and the commander of Oyapock was soon offering Monsier de Martel a pilot to help with navigation. Jean continued to travel in his own boat, and was then much moved when the Portuguese vessel eventually had to turn for home. He recorded the 'noble conduct' and 'fine attentions' received from de Martel, and left him 'with all the sentiments' which the man so well deserved, having been 'inspirational'. No one seemed to say, throughout this display of mutual enthusiasm, that everything might have proceeded much more smoothly had Jean Godin embarked with the Portuguese vessel some five years earlier. Certainly he omits to mention this point in the letter to his chief.

That date of 22 July 1770 needs to be set in the context of the story as a whole. Jean had set sail from La Rochelle thirty-five years earlier. Six years later he had married in Peru. Three years after that event his leader, La Condamine, had arrived at Cayenne. From 1749 to 1750 Jean had made his own Amazonian foray, this ending fifteen years after he had last seen France. The awful wait had then begun, with nothing truly positive happening for a further fifteen years and six months until the galiot's extraordinary arrival. Ten months later that same vessel dropped anchor at Lagunas. Three years and two months later still Isabela left home with her party of forty-one, only for terrible tragedy to strike. Ten months and twenty-two days after her departure from Riobamba she and her husband jointly reached Cayenne.

The time Jean had then spent with his 'darling wife' had been seven years and three months out of the twenty-eight years and five months since their wedding day. The young couple, aged thirteen and thirty on that happy occasion, had reached forty-one and fifty-eight by the time they were able to celebrate, once again, another start to life in each other's company. At that time they had been apart, separated by the width of a continent, for twenty-one years and four months. In their extraordinary, if distant, fashion they had been entirely loyal to their union for all that period. As for Jean's loyalty to France, and to his family there, he had been a youngster of twenty-three when he had left home. He was about to return rather more than middle-aged. In fact, with few in the eighteenth century reaching the psalmist's proclaimed threescore years and ten, he was then elderly.

Nevertheless he did not hurry. Perhaps he had become accustomed to a leisurely form of haste, but there were also scores to settle. In particular there was a lawsuit between himself and Tristan d'Oreasaval. The monk/ doctor/opportunist had failed to deliver Jean's letters, as instructed. He had consumed the accompanying money on his own account, and he had then disregarded the request to bring Don Pedro to Lagunas. None of that had stopped him from suing Jean 'for the 60 livres per month' wages, covering an eighteen-month period, which Jean had originally offered. If everything had gone to plan, if Isabela had received news more speedily of the galiot's attendance, and if she had not suffered so greatly, that expectation of a year and a half might have been correct for the entire episode. As it was, owing mainly to d'Oreasaval's over-casual delivery arrangements, the whole foray had taken three times as long.

After much deliberation the Superior Council of Cayenne ordered Tristan to account for the money entrusted to him. He could not do so, and in the end a compromise was reached. Jean Godin won without gain, and he penned a diatribe.

> This miserable man, after having abused my trust, after having caused the death of eight people, including the Indian who drowned, and all the misfortunes my wife had to endure, had used up all the income from the effects that I had entrusted with him, was insolvent, and I had no wish to add to my losses by feeding him in prison.

There is no further mention in Jean's account of Dr Rivals.

Presumably he and his companion returned to France from Cayenne as soon as they were able. Isabela's father, Don Pedro, was still of the party in Guiana. When surveying the route for his daughter he had not entertained the idea of journeying to France, but the loss of his sons had made Riobamba less appealing. There was still a son-in-law in that city, a Senor Savala, but no further mention of a daughter, Isabela's sister. Therefore she too must have died, leaving her father with no immediate descendants in Peru. His health had apparently suffered, perhaps from the journey, and it therefore seemed wisest for him to accompany his surviving daughter and her husband, now so happily reunited, back to France.

Jean's practice of pleading for assistance from officialdom did not end merely because his wife had now rejoined him. He was soon writing to the Duke of Praslin, Minister and Secretary of State.

> Both of us throw ourselves at your Grace's feet to beg for clemency. I am indebted to this colony's bank for 3,700 [presumably livres] . . . and we dare to beg your grace that it should be declared null and void. After so many misfortunes we find ourselves absolutely unable to fulfil that obligation. Please, your Lordship, be so good as to consider our hopeless situation, and both of us will never stop praying for your Grace's good health.
>
> Your Lordship's very humble and obedient servant.

There was an extra inconvenience, apart from penury. Isabela may have had a luxurious voyage down the Amazon, with nourishments arriving from every quarter, but she was still unwell even six months after her emergence from the forest. Despite treatments given to make her more cheerful she 'remained sad', as Jean lamented. She was also, one assumes, a rather different person in his eyes. Not only had her hair turned white, allegedly almost overnight due to her forest experience, but she had been twenty when he had left her and was now over twice that age. Each had to reacquaint themselves with the person they had married. Not only did Isabela have to recover from her ordeal, but adjust herself to a different situation, such as begging officialdom for money. High living in Peru had become a simpler lifestyle in Cayenne. Her father, prominent in Riobamba, was just an old man in Guiana. Jean was no longer the youthful husband she had known, and the switch in circumstance cannot have been easy, either for her or him.

They certainly let it take some time. The couple settled down at Oyapock. Before long they moved to Cayenne, allegedly because of Isabela's poor health. They still made no effort to return to France, and gradually let 1770 become 1773. There is no mention how they made their living, and the census of 1772 describes Jean as 'penurious', possessing only eleven slaves. On the other hand South America could be an easy place for achieving life's essentials – a roof, a sufficiency of food in appropriate variety, and easy labour from the omnipresent Indians.

The lack of urgency can seem remarkable, particularly with the inherited property back in France to be administered, but Isabela's condition was almost certainly the cause. Jean did not wish her to experience the rigours of a long sea voyage until the time was right.

It is also arguable that neither of them, but Isabela in particular, wished to encounter the adulation which their story had aroused. Every salon, so it is said, had learned of the South American adventure, this being so packed with its variety of ingredients. Above all, and more critical than all the other facets put together, the happening was a woman's story. How many other women, in all of history, had ever such a tale to tell? Whether the Godin fear of this resounding fame was a cause for their delay or not, or whether Isabela's health was the sole concern, the couple stayed on in French Guiana, being in no haste to return.

Meanwhile events elsewhere were changing the more stable world that Jean had known when embarking from La Rochelle. The capricious Louis XV had one more year to live when the Godins were ready to leave for France. Madame de Pompadour, his influential mistress, had died nine years before he did so. Her famous words – After us the deluge – were becoming increasingly prophetic. No one was then speaking of revolution, or of the possibility that Louis XV's grandson might pay the extreme price for earlier indulgence and mismanagement, but everyone spoke of turmoil. Over in North America the situation was also changing rapidly. The Boston Massacre, with four men killed by British troops, had occurred shortly after the Godins had arrived at Cayenne. The Boston Tea Party took place as they were leaving it, and the American War of Independence would start two years later. From a Frenchman's point of view, and from that of many others, the world was a markedly different place in 1773 to the state it had been in when a frigate named *Portefaix* had transported eleven 'savants' to South America in 1735. If revolution was not actually visualized, the possibility of increasing disruption was surely contemplated. As for Jean Godin, he makes no mention of apprehension, or politics, or likely chaos when waiting to embark. That was not his way.

He had reached the age of sixty-one by the time his party set sail for France on 21 April 1773. His father-in-law, Don Pedro, was then sixty-nine. Beating them both in years, after their sixty-five-day voyage across the Atlantic, was a frail seventy-two-year-old standing on the dock at La Rochelle to greet the arrivals. It was surely quite a trial for Charles-Marie de la Condamine to be at the quayside, as he was partly paralysed, extremely deaf, and would die six months afterwards. One account of his life states that his 'stream of books [occurred] despite a tropical disease which consumed his vitals'. The paralysis, which had begun sixteen years earlier, had started in his legs before spreading to his hands. In short, his later years had not been kind to him, but he had to be there at the quayside to witness the homecoming of the final member of his South American expedition which had set out from

173

there thirty-eight years earlier with such high hopes. His leader's responsibilities had been concluded and he could return to Paris, his mission having finally been accomplished. It is possible that this final act of loyalty to a colleague hastened his demise.

CHAPTER 12

The Chain-Bearer Comes Home

1773–92

It may have been a long time since Charles-Marie de la Condamine had last seen his chain-bearer, and it may also have been twenty-nine years since the expedition's leader had last experienced the continent of South America, but by no means did he forget either the continent or his former colleague. No galiot would ever have arrived at Cayenne had La Condamine not exerted his influence wherever possible, and upon whoever might be able to resolve the issue. As his stature had grown, both within scientific circles and at the Academy, his entreaties had become steadily more effective. When the political situation changed, his requests fell upon increasingly fertile ground, but nothing would have happened concerning poor Jean Godin and his isolation had the former leader not been diligent on his behalf.

For La Condamine the expedition had not been a fragment of his life, a passing event soon to be forgotten; it and its collected information became his sole concern. He

175

had spent only seven years on the southern continent, but he never really left it for his final thirty years. He became its general ambassador, its spokesman, its principal publicist. If anyone wished to know anything about South America they would contact him. Had he been the first, and only, traveller to another planet he could not have been more in demand. In biographies of La Condamine he is listed as scientist and traveller, but his travelling was limited to that single earth-measuring expedition. It alone had provided him with sufficient experience and recorded information to last a lifetime. (Charles Darwin, in the following century, would behave in similar fashion. Having voyaged for five years on the *Beagle* he then hardly left home for the remainder of his life, occupied with ideas sparked off by his circumnavigation.)

La Condamine had wasted no time in becoming the savant par excellence about South America. No sooner had he reached Paris back in 1745 than he had put pen to paper, not about science at first but about the fatal assault upon Dr Jean Senièrgues. It still rankled that the assailants had not been brought to justice, and *Lettre sur l'émeute populaire de Cuenca* put forward his views in stringent style. Nothing further then happened in connection with that 'popular insurrection', but the expedition leader had at least aired his grievances. More importantly he was next writing a summary of the entire trip, but this major work did not appear until 1751. *Journal du voyage fait par ordre du roi a l'équateur* made his name, along with his two other volumes of a more technical nature. His principal book's sub-title stated that it 'served as a historical introduction to the measurement of the meridian's first three degrees', but it was very much more than that. It was a full-scale introduction to the astonishments of South America, and it did astonish. Thenceforth an appetite grew among scientists everywhere to learn more of this new world, not least the Spanish and Portuguese who seem to have been taken by surprise at all the revelations. La Condamine and the Academy had been granted an opportunity to prize open South America's doors, and these were never to close again quite so rigidly.

Although the southern continent remained his dominant concern La Condamine was also forthright about the possibilities of smallpox vaccination (after he had witnessed its potential at Pará and, in part, because his own face had been scarred by *la petite vérole*). He fervently campaigned for a universal system of measurement, perhaps influenced by all the differing league lengths he had encountered on his travels. He argued successfully that the toise, this length equivalent to one fathom/six feet, should be adopted as a legal standard. Although the metre and the metric system would involve different lengths, when formally introduced later in that century, La Condamine had prepared the ground for their introduction, with everyone then appreciating that a universal approach to measurement was advantageous. Foreign academies – St Petersburg, Stockholm, Berlin – elected him to their ranks and, in 1760, so did the Académie Française. This organisation, founded in the seventeenth century, is far more prestigious than the Académie des Sciences, limiting itself to forty members known as the 'Immortals'.

It had been a supreme gesture on La Condamine's part to welcome the Godins home. His paralysis and deafness had been unwelcome partners to his life for so long, and were each severe by the time of the quayside arrival, with the famous scientist considering himself 'half a man' on that occasion. Certainly he was no longer capable of writing. He had married a niece in 1757 when aged fifty-six. The papal dispensation for such a close relationship was achieved when La Condamine, on holiday in Italy for his health, personally visited the Vatican. His young wife helped him greatly during their seventeen years together, as South America continued to dominate his life and work. The ardent curiosity never left him.

A rival in such knowledge might have been Pedro Maldonado, the fellow voyager down the Amazon who then chose to live in Paris. He too became an *académicien*, and was also elected to other learned societies. When Britain's Royal Society made him a Fellow, he travelled to London to be present at his election. The Peruvian who had suffered and survived so many South American perils then caught measles, and this disease vanquished him at the age of forty. La Condamine therefore became the undisputed leader in his field until his death. La Condamine was the first to portray the New World scientifically. His books prompted Alexander von Humboldt to travel there for five years and Humboldt's lifetime of writings caused a further deluge, of British and German naturalists in particular, to explore the place.

After that La Rochelle reunion Jean, Isabela and her father travelled to St Amand Montrond (or Mont Rond) in Cher, 140 direct miles south of Paris. Human separation was often lengthy in the eighteenth century, when men went off to war or on administrative postings overseas, but Jean Godin's thirty-eight years was exceptional and there was much for him to learn on his return home. His father, as he knew, had died in 1740, and his mother had done likewise eleven years later, shortly after Jean had started his lengthy sojourn in Cayenne. His only brother had died even before the expedition had begun, and two widowed sisters were the closest relations able to greet him at his home. They were both effusive over his arrival and in their acceptance of another woman in the house-hold, the famous Isabela. As the single surviving male Jean was well placed to take over and look after the family's concerns. It is arguable that he should have accepted this responsibility a great deal earlier, rather than letting time pass by in French Guiana, but he had considered his greater duty lay in waiting for his wife to come down-stream.

La Condamine had not only welcomed the safe return of his final colleague, but had requested that a royal pension should be granted. For anyone to work half a dozen years, to marry locally, to abandon that new home in Peru, and so mismanage things that a twenty-year separation ensues as a direct result, this period often supported by government funding, might make a pension seem over-generous, but La Condamine was happy to arrange it and Jean was happy to accept the '700 livres per year, net 630 livres', granted on 27 October 1773. In the letter of gratitude to his dying leader Jean wrote that his wife was now 'au sein de ma famille', and had been 'received with tenderness'.

As for Isabela her travails in the forest left their scars. She suffered from a nervous tic, which apparently became more serious whenever she was asked about her 'adventure'. One early chronicler of her story called it a 'souvenir' of those terrible times. She would also, on occasion, tremble in the dark. As tics often result from emotional stress it is thoroughly understandable that she should suffer from them. Her skin had also deteriorated, being blotchy (*tavelée*), and never regaining its former state. Insect bites were thought to have been responsible. Her smile was described as '*mélancholique*', and her manner was similar. Physically she was in France, but much of her was still back in South America. On occasion, and when alone, she would open a small ebony box. This contained the soles of the shoes she had cut from her dead brother in the forest, and also the cloth which the Andoas Indian women had given her to hide her nakedness. The forest tragedy, and its extraordinary survival, had happened three and a half years before Isabela Godin arrived at St Amand, but it was never lightly pushed aside, as some can do with terrible events. With her it stayed supreme.

Jean and Isabela moved into the family house on Rue de l'Hotel-Dieu. For a time the two of them worked on a Quecha-French dictionary, and also on a Quecha grammar. French was much of the world's lingua franca, and so was Quecha around the Andes, but such books would have had little general appeal, mainly because the Andean region was wholly Spanish. In any case it does not appear that either volume was completed. Jean also continued his promotional work, advocating a greater interest by France in commercial possibilities around the Amazon. In particular, as with a letter written on 30 October 1774, he stressed how very cheaply cows could be obtained from Pará. Thirteen years later another letter showed that he was pursuing the same topic with identical argument. Jean Godin may not have had a tic, but he too twitched in similar style when thinking of South America.

Isabela and Jean were no longer able to have children, but an addition to their family occurred when Jean-Antoine arrived from Peru. His father had been Antoine, one of Isabela's two brothers who had perished in the forest. This son also preferred the thought of living in France, and therefore moved in with his grandfather, aunt and uncle at St Amand. In time he married a local girl, Magdeleine Picot, but his arrival in France had not been a total happiness, mainly for being at odds with Isabela and Jean when they refused to pay for his education. (It is difficult to know how much money might have been involved, mainly for not knowing Jean-Antoine's age when he arrived.)

Seven years after his arrival in France Don Pedro died. This long-time widower, already called shadowy, became yet more insubstantial when living in France. The shock of learning that two sons, a daughter, and a grandson had all died, and then the further shock of that daughter's reappearance, coupled with her account of the forest horror, had left him unbalanced, and he never acquired his former composure. For his final years he is said to have existed in a 'reverie', half back in the splendour he had previously known in Peru. At all events he died on 28 November 1780. By that time Jean's two widowed sisters had also died.

Jean Godin's royal pension was 'suppressed' in 1789, the year of revolution. No longer did he write to the government about cattle, timber, or whatever took his fancy, but worked primarily with the lands that were his inheritance. Then, on 1 March 1792, he too died at his home on the Rue de l'Hotel-Dieu at the age of seventy-nine. He therefore topped and tailed his life equally at St Amand, spending his first nineteen years there and then the final nineteen. Almost half of his years were passed in South America, most of them unwillingly.

Isabela Godin followed him on 28 September in that same year of 1792, aged sixty-six. One wonders whether the turmoil of those revolutionary times contributed to their ends, and one certainly wonders whether Jean's departure hastened that of his widow. Their union, so lengthily disrupted, had astonished the world when its tale was told. It therefore seems correct, however sad, that both partners took their leave of life in the self-same year.

As for their inheritance from Jean's father, the couple possessed no descendants, so the property was inherited by the disgruntled Jean-Antoine, Isabela's nephew, whose education had not been paid for. He and Magdeleine had married two weeks before Jean's death. They set up home on the rue du Cheval Blanc and had three children, but only one survived. This youngster was Gilbert Félix de Grandmaison y Bruno, and with him this story is at its end. He was then the owner of the Godin property at Epourneaux, acquired by Jean's father between 1735 and 1740. (Other Godin properties were then possessed by other branches of the wider Godin family.) At Epourneaux Félix constructed a 'model educational establishment', and with his marriage he too had one son, le Docteur Emmanuel de Grandmaison y Bruno. Even though the direct line of the family then moved from St Amand and the district of Berry to Neuilly-sur-Seine near Paris this man, more than anyone else, inherited the story of his great-great-uncle and great-great-aunt, the famous pair who, for much of the eighteenth century, provided the world with a tale, the like of which it had never heard before.

A Personal Epilogue

As with many good things in life I encountered the Godin story by accident. It had been my fortune to spend much time on the River Amazon, travelling within its colossal basin loosely known as Amazonia. After a while it had annoyed me that I knew so little about its human history, which European had first voyaged down it, who had been first to go up, who had produced its first map, and so on. By contrast such facts about the River Nile seem to arrive our way almost, as it were, with our mother's milk. When do we each first learn of Speke and Burton, Livingstone, Baker and Grant, or General Gordon and then Kitchener of Khartoum? It must be extremely early, and a great deal earlier than Orellana, Aguirre, Teixeira, and then La Condamine. Perhaps – dread thought – this is solely because the Nile discoverers were British, and those going up or down the Amazon were, well, foreign.

While I was reading about Charles-Marie de la Condamine, the French savant who pioneered science upon the Amazon, who brought back rubber and curare to Europe, and who inspired a host of others to go travelling in his steps, I first encountered Monsieur and Madame Godin des Odonais and the story of their separation. Of course I was intrigued. Fancy waiting in Cayenne for such a lengthy period! And what an ordeal Isabela experienced during her effort to be reunited with the individual she had last seen twenty years earlier!

I soon learned they had ended their days at a spot in France called St Amand Montrond. On the map I saw it existed on the River Cher just where the flat countryside to its north starts growing contours to its south. It looked nice for a visit, and I wondered if its citizens knew of a particular couple who, after spending time in South America during the eighteenth century, had finally lived and died in St Amand. If this sounds presumptuous, or even rude, try asking Brazilians about their knowledge or experience concerning the mighty Amazon. Within atlases this single river seems to dominate their country, but most Brazilians have never set foot within its colossal basin or encountered any of its water, despite it being the most massive of all the rivers in the world.

I thought, in connection with St Amand, that I would first telephone its libary. Librarians tend to be good on history and local knowledge, and those by the Cher would inform me if the name of Godin meant anything to anyone today. Therefore, as is my custom before launching into French, I prepared a few sentences which would probably come in handy. 'Have you ever heard of a couple named Godin des Odonais?' 'Do you know a historian who might help me with this name?' 'Do you know a historian who might know other historians who might know?' That last was troublesome even in English but, in essence, my questions came down to a single query: '*Connaissez-vous le nom Isabela Godin des Odonais, s'il vous plait?*'

The French have a way of confounding us with their answers. They never seem to say what we are hoping they will say, such as '*Oui*' or '*Non*' when replying to our questioning. As if applying a single finger to a machine gun's trigger they produce a flurry, a torrent, an avalanche of words in immediate reply. We listen eagerly, hoping to catch their drift, but puzzle internally whether the answer is a positive or a negative. As if trying to grab a single machine gun bullet as it hurtles by, and failing, we soon resort to the fundamental point. '*Excusez-moi; votre résponse est oui où non?*'

The library at St Amand was to floor me utterly, but not in standard fashion. Scarcely had I dialled the number than a click indicated the connection had been made. Drawing in breath I started to deliver, but they delivered first. '*Bibliothèque Isabel Godin ici*,' said the voice, expressing it all almost as a single word.

My breath vanished instantly. So did all my sentences. Like a fish upon the bank I only opened and closed my mouth, but a relationship with St Amand had begun. From then on, after an initial five minutes of linguistic floundering, and with numerous improvisations failing to hit the mark, it was progress all the way. Eventually I was ending with '*Oui, j'arrive*', as Napoleon allegedly used to scribble in post-war notes to Josephine before adding: '*Ne lave pas.*' I left it that I would arrive, and discarded the bit about not washing. Merely arriving would plainly be sufficient entertainment.

From the railway station, as it seemed a fair hike to the *centre du ville*, I took a taxi. '*Bibliothéque-Isabel-Godin, s'il-vous plâit,*' I demanded, favouring the one-word technique I hoped might show me as a native.

It worked. A sign flashed by stating that St Amand Montrond was twinned with Riobamba. I smiled. And there it was, with the lettering quite clear:

BIBLIOTHÉQUE MUNICIPALE

CENTRE CULTUREL ISABEL GODIN

Inside that building, most charmingly, I was made to feel the hero of the hour, and then of the days that followed. A great gathering of Godin enthusiasts, relations, and Godin society members were there to welcome me. They showered me with booklets, information, photocopies. I received items published by the Association Berry-Chimborazo which operates from the Centre Culturel Isabel Godin on the Cours Manuel in St Amand. These told me of the close ties with Ecuador, and how citizens of Riobamba and St Amand travel to each other's lands. The library informants spoke of the cemeteries where the Godins had been buried, and they certainly ushered me towards a bronze bust of their city's most famous heroine erect upon a plinth within the city's Square Fleurus, her head and shoulders sculpted by Fabien Lattoré of Ecuador in 1988.

On my way I passed the house on the Rue de l'Hotel Dieu occupied by the Godins during their final years. It possessed a plaque on its outside wall to inform all passers-by of St Amand's most famous citizens.

Isabelle de Casa Mayor
Jean Godin des Odonais, membre de
l'Expédition de la Condamine a
Équateur ont acheve ici leur
vie d'Aventure en 1792

This famous home is now occupied by the Jeanne d'Arc primary school.

To all people of St Amand, so helpful, kind and enthusiastic, I am indebted for the substance of this book. I am also delighted that my first, well prepared French sentence had never in fact been used. '*Connaissez-vous le nom Godin des Odonais?*'

What a travesty that would have been!

Anthony Smith
London

Index

191

Index

Index

Index